CHEMISTRY (INTERMEDIATE 2)
Contents of mandatory course units

(a) Substances

Elements

- There are just over 100 elements in the world of chemistry.

- Most elements are found naturally but some, like plutonium, are man-made in nuclear reactors.

- Most elements are metals. Metals are good conductors of electricity and heat.

- Most of the elements are solids at normal temperature.

- There are only two liquid elements at normal temperature, mercury (a metal) and bromine (a non-metal).

- Only eleven of the elements are gases.

- Each element has its own name and its own chemical symbol.

- Some symbols e.g. C for carbon, are single capital letters while others e.g. Li for lithium, are double letters (the first one is a capital).

- The most recently discovered elements are being given three-letter symbols e.g. the element unnilquadium has the symbol Unq.

- Many names and symbols are derived from Latin or Greek e.g. Pb *plumbum*, Au *aurum* (Latin); Br *bromos*, I *iodes* (Greek).

- Symbols He, Ne, Ar, Kr and Xe are all derived from Greek words i.e. *helios* 'sun', *neos* 'new', *argos* 'inert', *kryptos* 'hidden', *xenos* 'stranger'.

- Man-made elements are named after planets, places or very famous scientists e.g. Np for neptunium; Cf for californium; Cm for curium; Es for einsteinium.

The Periodic Table

- In 1829, the German chemist Döbereiner noticed that some three-element sets (called triads) showed similar chemical properties e.g. Cl, Br, I; Ca, Sr, Ba; Fe, Co, Mn, etc.

- In 1864, the English chemist Newlands showed that when the early elements were placed in the order of their increasing atomic weights, repeating chemical properties appeared at every eighth place (called the law of octaves).

- These attempts to reveal patterns within the chemical properties of the elements were taken further by the independent, pioneering investigations of the German chemist Meyer and the Russian chemist Mendeleev which laid the foundations for our modern form of the Periodic Table of the Elements.

- All the known elements are listed by symbol in the chart familiarly called the Periodic Table.

- Horizontal rows of elements are called Periods.

- Vertical rows of elements are called Groups.

- All the elements in a Group of the Periodic Table possess similar chemical properties.

- Some Groups are known by names which relate to these chemical properties.

- Group 1 ('Alkali Metals') are very reactive metals which are stored under light oil.

- Group 7 ('Halogens') - the name means '*salt producers*' - are very reactive non-metals.

- Group 0 ('Noble Gases') are extremely unreactive gases.

- The 'Transition Metals' lie between Groups 2 and 3.

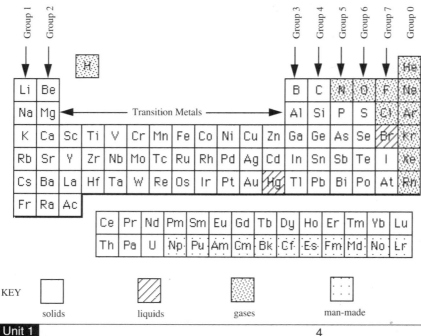

Periodic Table of Elements showing some classification categories

KEY: solids | liquids | gases | man-made

CHEMISTRY
course notes
2
INTERMEDIATE

Sandy Herd

**Formerly, Principal Teacher of Chemistry
Kirkland High School & Community College**

and

Chris Sparling

**Formerly, Principal Teacher of Chemistry
Dunfermline High School**

© *Copyright* 1999 A. Herd & C. Sparling

ISBN 1-898890-27-7

Published by
Leckie & Leckie Ltd, 8 Whitehill Terrace, St Andrews, Scotland, KY16 8RN
tel: 01334 475656 fax: 01334 477392
email: s.leckie@leckie-and-leckie.co.uk web: www.leckie-and-leckie.co.uk

Authors' thanks to our families

A CIP Catalogue record for this book is available from the British Library.

Printed in Scotland by Inglis Allen on environmentally-friendly paper. The paper is made from a mixture of sawmill waste, forest thinnings and wood from sustainable forests.

Leckie & Leckie

CHEMISTRY (INTERMEDIATE 2)
A course outline

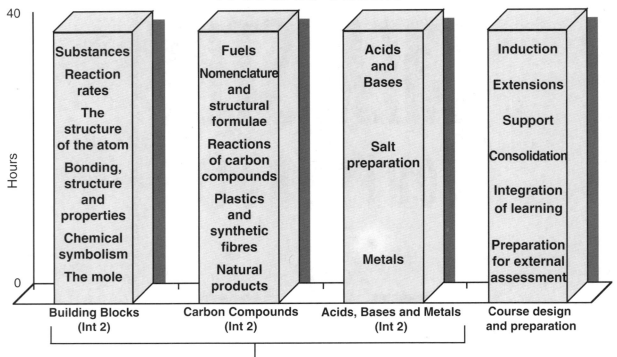

Three mandatory units

The notes in this publication describe the knowledge and understanding associated with the mandatory units of your course:

Unit 1	**Building Blocks (Int 2)**
Unit 2	**Carbon Compounds (Int 2)**
Unit 3	**Acids, Bases and Metals (Int 2)**

In addition to carrying out regular course practical work to illustrate the course content in these three units, you will also be expected to carry out the **prescribed practical activities** listed below:

- Effect of concentration on the rate of reactions (Unit 1)
- Effect of temperature on the rate of reactions (Unit 1)
- Electrolysis (Unit 1)
- Testing for unsaturation (Unit 2)
- Cracking (Unit 2)
- Hydrolysis of starch (Unit 2)
- Preparation of a salt (Unit 3)
- Factors which affect voltage (Unit 3)
- Reactions of metals with oxygen (Unit 3)

Chemical points relating to each of these practical activities are also dealt with in these notes.

A brief note from the authors

A number of you entering this course of study will have already been studying chemistry at either Standard Grade or at Intermediate level 1. Others may have been studying Biology or Physics at either Standard Grade or Intermediate level 2, or even Science at Standard Grade.

*Whatever your previous experiences, you should be aware that this CHEMISTRY(Int 2) course builds on your achievements in **knowledge and understanding**, **problem solving** and **practical skills** from these previous studies.*

You will see from the sub-topic headings for each unit (column chart above) that many of these will extend and develop areas of chemistry which you may have already encountered in courses of chemistry from previous years but do not be concerned if this is your first opportunity to meet the subject of chemistry. You can be sure that your knowledge and understanding of scientific concepts from your previous courses will provide you with a sound foundation to build success in this chemistry course.

We both experienced school chemistry and then worked in chemical industries while continuing part-time studies to HNC level. Eventually, we studied chemistry full-time to honours degree level.

As teachers of chemistry for many years, we have maintained our enthusiasm for this - our favourite - subject!

We hope that you will enjoy undertaking your chemistry studies supported by our course notes which we have presented in a style and topic order to assist your learning of chemistry.

Sandy Herd & Chris Sparling

Uses of elements

It would take quite a list to include even one use for each of the 100+ known elements, so here is a selection:

- Hydrogen, H, - to make ammonia, NH_3, and methanol, CH_3OH, very important industrial chemicals, and in margarine production.

- Helium, He, - in balloons and dirigibles and as part of the gas mixture for under-water divers to breathe.

- Fluorine, F, - to make the non-stick plastic called Teflon™ and aerosol CFCs.

- Neon, Ne, - in lighting tubes for advertising displays and in gas lasers.

- Sodium, Na, - a cooling agent in some types of nuclear reactor.

- Magnesium, Mg, - in fireworks and flares.

- Oxygen, O, - as liquid fuel in some rockets and missiles.

- Platinum, Pt, - in jewellery and in catalysts fitted to car exhaust systems.

- Aluminium, Al, - in aircraft construction and in 'ring-pull' soft drinks cans.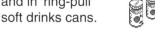

- Silicon, Si, - in transistors and in computer chips for the electronics industries.

- Chlorine, Cl, - for bleaching paper and for killing germs in drinking water supplies.

- Argon, Ar, - in gas lasers and in electric filament light bulbs.

- Copper, Cu, - in electrical wiring and cables, in electric motors and generators, and in coins.

- Zinc, Zn, - to galvanise steel (anti-corrosion).

- Gold, Au, - in jewellery, as currency bars and even as fillings in teeth (dentistry).

- Phosphorus, P, - in safety matches.

Reactions of the Group 1 elements

- These metals are so soft in comparison to most metals, they can be cut easily with a knife.
  (Teacher/lecturer demonstration!)

- The Group 1 elements or Alkali Metals react readily with the oxygen in air and must be kept under light oil to avoid this happening.

- The metallic elements combine with oxygen (~20 % air by volume) to form compounds called metal oxides.

  lithium   + oxygen ⟶ lithium oxide

  sodium   + oxygen ⟶ sodium oxide

  potassium   + oxygen ⟶ potassium oxide

- The Group 1 elements have violent reactions with cold water. (Teacher/lecturer demonstration!) **Explosive**

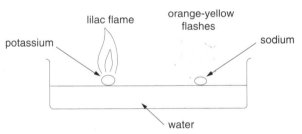

- The metallic elements react violently with the cold water forming hydrogen gas and alkaline solutions of metal hydroxides.

  potassium + water ⟶ hydrogen + potassium hydroxide

  sodium + water ⟶ hydrogen + sodium hydroxide

Making and naming compounds

- The simplest compounds contain only two elements joined together by chemical bonds.
  e.g. copper + chlorine ⟶ copper chloride

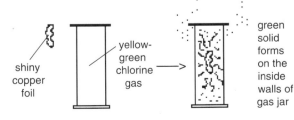

shiny copper foil   yellow-green chlorine gas   green solid forms on the inside walls of gas jar

- Most compounds with names ending in '–ide' have only two elements combined (hydroxides are an exception!)
  e.g. sodium chloride, NaCl, contains sodium and chlorine.

- Methane (carbon hydride), CH_4, contains carbon and hydrogen.

- Compounds whose names end in '–ite' or in '–ate' also contain the element oxygen joined with the other elements indicated in the name.

Chemical Reactions

- Chemical reactions are not confined to the school laboratory! They occur in everyday life!

  - cooking foods

  - burning fuel in a car engine

  - striking a match

  - setting candles alight on a birthday cake

  - 'hardening' of epoxy glues

- When chemicals are mixed together, they do not always react e.g. sand and sugar together just produce a mixture of the two solids!

- When a chemical reaction does take place, there may be one, or more, new substances formed.

- The starting chemicals in reactions are called reactants and any new substances formed are called products.

- When chemical reactions take place, there may be one, or more, of the following:

  - a colour change

  - the appearance of a solid (a precipitate)

  - a fizzing as a gas forms

  - a temperature change

- Some chemical reactions are only identified by either an increase or a decrease in the temperature of the surroundings showing that energy changes are taking place.

Mixtures

- Mixtures occur when substances are put together but do not react.

- Grey iron filings (a metal) stirred with yellow sulphur powder (a non-metal) do not react on mixing.

- Substances in a mixture can be separated. e.g.

Fe and S mixture

The magnetic property of Fe enables it to be separated by attraction to the magnet

yellow sulphur

- Paper chromatography can separate quite complex mixtures!

dye mixture spotted on shaped filter paper disk

coloured bands on filter paper show the number of components in the dye mixture

petri dish 'tank' with meths/water solvent

- In exothermic reactions, energy is released from the chemical system into the immediate surroundings. This causes an experimentally observable increase in temperature. e.g. acid/alkali reactions

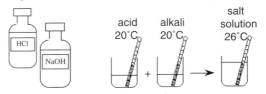

- To reach 20 °C again, the hot salt solution, which is the product, must release heat energy to the surroundings. The chemical products of any exothermic reaction will thus end up having less chemical energy than the chemical reactants.

- In endothermic reactions, energy is absorbed by the chemical system from the immediate surroundings. This causes an experimentally observable decrease in temperature. e.g. dissolving ammonium nitrate in water

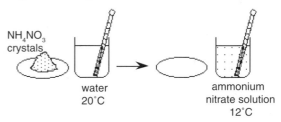

NH_4NO_3 crystals

water 20°C

ammonium nitrate solution 12°C

- To reach 20 °C again, the cool ammonium nitrate solution, which is the product, must absorb heat energy from the surroundings. The chemical products of any endothermic reaction will thus end up having more chemical energy than the chemical reactants.

- Air is a mixture of several gases which form the Earth's atmosphere.

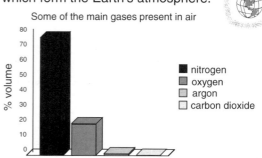

Some of the main gases present in air

- nitrogen
- oxygen
- argon
- carbon dioxide

- Oxygen gas relights a glowing splint and this is used as an identification test for oxygen. (There is insufficient oxygen in air for this test to be positive.)

- Air cooled under pressure can be liquefied and separated by fractional distillation. This depends on the liquefied gases in the mixture having different boiling points e.g. nitrogen boils at −196 °C while oxygen boils at the slightly higher temperature of −183 °C.

Solutions

- Solutions are mixtures formed when solutes (solids) dissolve in liquids (solvents).

- Such solids which dissolve in liquids are said to be soluble e.g. common salt (NaCl) is very soluble in water.

- A solute which does not dissolve in a solvent is said to be insoluble e.g. candle wax, which is completely insoluble in water.

- State symbols can be applied to substances if required:

  (s) = solid;   (g) = gas
  (l) = liquid;   (aq) = aqueous solution
                                (water as solvent)

  e.g. the dissolving of ammonium nitrate in water may appear as the chemical equation:

  $$NH_4NO_3(s) + H_2O(l) \longrightarrow NH_4NO_3(aq)$$

- If a solute is added to a solvent until no more solute can dissolve, the solution prepared is said to be saturated ('full up').

- Chemists can describe the concentration of a solution in $g\ dm^{-3}$ (i.e. grams of dissolved solute per cubic decimetre of solution, where $1\ dm^3 = 1000\ cm^3$).

- A solution containing $1\ g\ dm^{-3}$ of a solute with a solubility of $15\ g\ dm^{-3}$ may be described as a dilute solution.

- A solution of this solid containing $13\ g\ dm^{-3}$ may be described as a concentrated solution.

- A solution is diluted to a lower concentration by the addition of more solvent.

- When an aqueous solution is carefully heated, the dissolved solid (solute) is recovered by evaporating water (solvent) from the solution.

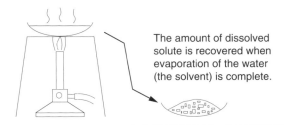

The amount of dissolved solute is recovered when evaporation of the water (the solvent) is complete.

(b) Reaction rates

Following the course of a reaction

- Chemical reactions occur at different rates.

- Explosions are the result of extremely fast chemical reactions!

- Some reactions are slow e.g. the rusting of a steel bridge.

- Some chemical reactions are very slow and go almost unnoticed!

- Moderately fast reactions, lasting several minutes, are most useful for chemistry laboratory rate studies.

- Chemical reaction rate studies may follow the change in concentration of either reactant(s) or product(s) over a period of time.

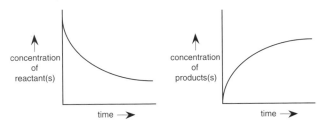

- A fast reaction (one which has a high rate) will take place in a shorter time than a reaction of lower rate.

 Reaction stage completed in 12 s – higher reaction rate   Reaction stage completed in 52 s – lower reaction rate

- The course of the reaction between calcium carbonate and hydrochloric acid giving $CO_2(g)$ can be followed by monitoring the change in mass of the reaction container at regular time intervals.

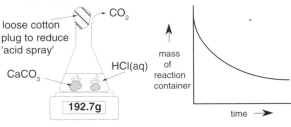

- The course of the reaction between calcium carbonate and hydrochloric acid can also be followed by measuring the changes in volume of the gaseous product over a period of time.

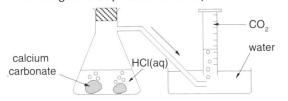

- The rate of a reaction is fastest at the start and decreases with time.

- The relative steepness of a stage in the graph is an indication of the reaction rate at that time.

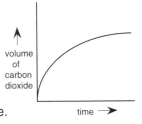

You should be able to describe a selection of reaction rate experiments and be able to handle tables of results and to draw and interpret graphs from information gathered during investigations.

Calculating the average rate of reaction

- The average rate of a reaction or any stage in a reaction is related to $1/t$ (t = time).

$$\text{Average rate} = \frac{\text{change in concentration}}{\text{time}}$$

- Rate units are $mol\ dm^{-3}\ s^{-1}$ (moles per cubic decimetre per second).

Consider an experiment where the concentration of reactant A is being monitored:

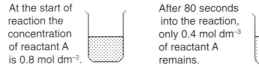

At the start of reaction the concentration of reactant A is $0.8\ mol\ dm^{-3}$.

After 80 seconds into the reaction, only $0.4\ mol\ dm^{-3}$ of reactant A remains.

$$\text{Average rate for this stage} = \frac{\text{change in concentration}}{\text{time}}$$

$$= \frac{0.8 - 0.4}{80}$$

$$= \frac{0.4}{80} = 0.005\ mol\ dm^{-3}\ s^{-1}$$

- The average rates of reaction at different stages can be calculated from graphs. e.g.

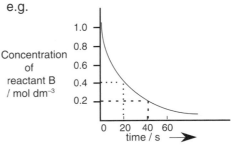

$$\text{Average rate over first 20 s} = \frac{\text{change in concentration}}{\text{time}}$$

$$= \frac{1.0 - 0.4}{20}$$

$$= \frac{0.6}{20} = 0.03\ mol\ dm^{-3}\ s^{-1}$$

$$\text{Average rate over next 20 s} = \frac{\text{change in concentration}}{\text{time}}$$

$$= \frac{0.4 - 0.2}{20}$$

$$= \frac{0.2}{20} = 0.01\ mol\ dm^{-3}\ s^{-1}$$

Collision theory

- Collision theory is based on the idea that, before any chemical reaction can take place, the reactant particles must have enough energy to collide together in such a way as to form products.
- The minimum amount of energy needed to bring about a chemical reaction is often referred to as the 'activation energy'.

- Not all collisions between particles – which may be atoms, molecules or ions – result in a chemical reaction. Sometimes the colliding particles deal each other no more than a glancing blow or they simply bounce apart completely unaffected!
- The effect on the rate of a chemical reaction by changing such things as the concentration, the particle size or the temperature of a set of chemical reactants can be explained in terms of the collision theory.

Factors affecting rate of reaction

Change in concentration (other variables constant)

- Concentrations of acids and other chemical solutions are expressed in moles per cubic decimetre (usually written as $mol\ dm^{-3}$).
- $2\ mol\ dm^{-3}\ HCl(aq)$ has twice the number of particles in solution as $1\ mol\ dm^{-3}\ HCl(aq)$.
- In separate $HCl(aq)/CaCO_3$ reactions using these acids, more collisions are possible on the surfaces of calcium carbonate lumps with the $2\ mol\ dm^{-3}\ HCl(aq)$.

- Increasing the concentration of one chemical causes the rate of collisions between the reactant particles to increase.
- The number of successful collisions will also increase giving rise to an increase in the rate of the chemical reaction.

- In $HCl(aq)/CaCO_3$ reactions, the volume of CO_2 obtained depends on which reactant is in excess.

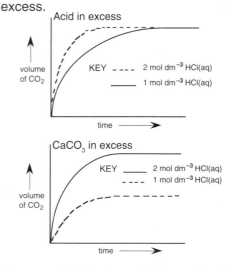

- For most chemical reactions, rate is directly proportional to concentration of reactant(s).

Factors affecting rate of reaction

Change in particle size (other variables constant)

- A lump of calcium carbonate cut into smaller pieces has a greater surface area exposed on which many more collisions can take place when it reacts with HCl(aq).

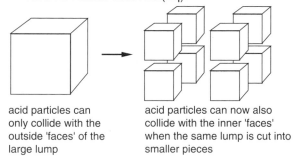

acid particles can only collide with the outside 'faces' of the large lump

acid particles can now also collide with the inner 'faces' when the same lump is cut into smaller pieces

- The reaction is over very quickly when very small lumps of calcium carbonate are used and powdered calcium carbonate can often react too quickly for measurements to be taken in a laboratory rate study experiment!

- Using smaller lumps of $CaCO_3$, with a mass twice that of a large lump of $CaCO_3$, will not only give a faster rate but will produce twice the volume of gas.

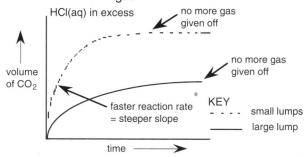

- Reducing the particle size of a solid reactant increases the surface area in contact, thus increasing the number of successful collisions with other reactant particles. This results in an increase in the rate of reaction.

- As particle size ↓, surface area ↑ and rate ↑.

Change in temperature (other variables constant)

- When chemical solutions are heated up, the particles present move around at a greater speed i.e. they have more kinetic energy.

- This increase in temperature increases the chances of the particles colliding successfully and therefore increases the rate of reaction.

- Reactions between lump calcium carbonate and HCl(aq) at different temperatures gave the following results:

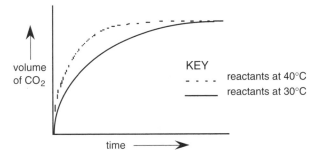

- A colourless sodium thiosulphate solution on mixing with dilute hydrochloric acid gradually becomes more 'cloudy yellow' due to sulphur forming in the mixture. Very soon, it becomes impossible to see through the 'cloudy yellow' mixture.

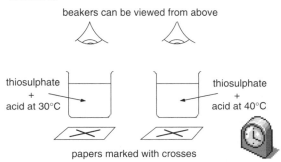

- The sulphur formation at 40 °C is much faster than the same reaction at 30 °C and obscures the 'paper cross' from the experimenter in a much shorter time.

- As temperature ↑, reaction rate ↑.

Some everyday chemical reactions and rate variables

While you were performing your rate investigations with a range of laboratory chemicals, some involving colour changes and bubbling gases, did you ever think once about chemical reactions in the home? Just think of all the chemical reactions which take place in, of all things, the chip pan – and the changes which must be taking place to the 'reactants' during chip-making! What a complicated set of reactions!

Here are a few simpler everyday situations for you to think about – you should be able to see how these relate to changes in the concentration or the particle size or the temperature of the 'reactants' involved!

- Potatoes cut into smaller pieces for boiling in water are 'ready' long before boiled whole potatoes.

- Fabric cleaning machines recommend the use of different numbers of capfuls of fluid per tank of water for the cleaning of different items.

- Carrots remain usable for a much longer period when stored in a refrigerator rather than a kitchen-unit vegetable drawer.

- The barbecue fire is usually set alight using the smallest charcoal lumps in the bag with bigger lumps being kept for adding later.

Catalysts

- Catalysts are chemical substances which can increase the speed of chemical reactions.

- A catalyst is not 'used up' during reaction and can be recovered chemically unchanged at the end of the reaction.

- Catalysts, which may be solids, liquids or gases, feature in many industrial processes.

- Small lumps of iron (Fe) are used as the catalyst in the industrial Haber Process for making ammonia (NH_3) from nitrogen (N_2) and hydrogen (H_2).

- Vanadium pentoxide (V_2O_5) is the catalyst used in the manufacture of sulphuric acid, and the conversion of vegetable oils to margarine requires a nickel (Ni) catalyst.

- In industries, catalysts allow reactions to take place at a lower temperature to save energy and, of course, save money!

- In homogeneous catalysis, the catalyst has the same physical state as the reactants. e.g. pink Co^{2+}(aq) in the laboratory reaction of H_2O_2(aq) with potassium sodium tartrate solution where the colour changes from pink to green and back to pink again, show that the Co^{2+}(aq) catalyst has been 'regenerated'.

- The catalyst has a different physical state from the reactants in heterogeneous catalysis. e.g. solid manganese dioxide catalyses the decomposition of hydrogen peroxide solution.

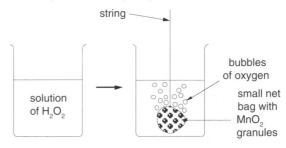

hydrogen peroxide ——> oxygen + water

Catalyst surfaces at work

- Solid catalysts provide 'active sites' on their surfaces to which reactant molecules are adsorbed.

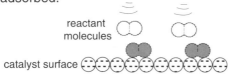

- Molecules adsorbed at 'active sites' are held in such a way that the internal bonds in these molecules are weakened allowing them to undergo collisions with the other reactant molecules more readily.

- Reaction takes place at the surface–

then the product molecules leave the 'active sites'.

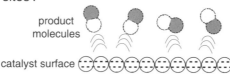

- Catalyst surfaces are said to be poisoned when 'active sites' are occupied by reactant impurities e.g. compounds of arsenic poison the V_2O_5 catalyst used in the Contact Process for the industrial production of sulphuric acid.

- Normally, catalysts can undergo regeneration to remove these reactant impurities but, if seriously poisoned, catalysts may require to be renewed.

- Catalytic converters are now fitted to the car exhaust systems of most new cars so that they can convert poisonous emission gases such as oxides of nitrogen (NO_x) and carbon monoxide (CO) to the safe, non-toxic gases nitrogen (N_2) and carbon dioxide (CO_2).

- Converters in cars can be made of platinum/ palladium/rhodium – transistion metals – with very large surface areas (to give a maximum number of 'active sites') but they must be used with 'lead-free' petrol to avoid poisoning of the catalyst and, thus, a reduction in its surface activity.

- If cheaper metals like Cu and Ni were used to make catalytic convertors it is quite likely that their surfaces would be poisoned more readily requiring their replacement sooner than Pt/Pd/Rh convertors. Ni reacts with CO.

Enzymes – biological catalysts

- Chemical reactions in animal and plant cells are catalysed by enzymes, which are now used in a number of industrial processes.

- Enzymes are efficient catalysts, most being very specific which means that a particular enzyme catalyses a particular reaction or type of reaction e.g. zymase in yeast produces ethanol from fermented carbohydrates.

- The enzyme invertase converts sucrose to glucose and fructose.

- Production of these monosaccharides by this method is now on an industrial scale such is the demand for them in the production of sweets and confectionery items.

(c) The structure of the atom

Sub-atomic particles

- All elements are made up of very small particles of matter called atoms.

- Each element contains atoms of the same kind (see isotopes later).

- The structure of an atom:

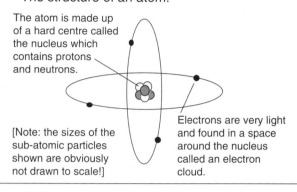

The atom is made up of a hard centre called the nucleus which contains protons and neutrons.

Electrons are very light and found in a space around the nucleus called an electron cloud.

[Note: the sizes of the sub-atomic particles shown are obviously not drawn to scale!]

Important numbers

- Atoms of different elements are very different in size and mass because they have different numbers of sub-atomic particles present.

- Atoms of different elements have their own unique number called the atomic number.

- The atomic number of an atom is equal to the number of protons in the nucleus of the atom.

- The atomic number of an atom actually gives two pieces of information about the atom:
  (a) the number of protons present, and
  (b) the number of electrons present.

- Electrons orbiting the nucleus, in the electron clouds, are arranged in a 'pattern' of energy levels or electron shells.

- Atoms can be imagined as small spheres with their energy levels or electron shells looking like layers of onion skin.

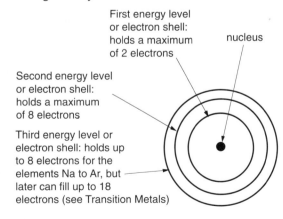

First energy level or electron shell: holds a maximum of 2 electrons

nucleus

Second energy level or electron shell: holds a maximum of 8 electrons

Third energy level or electron shell: holds up to 8 electrons for the elements Na to Ar, but later can fill up to 18 electrons (see Transition Metals)

- Chemists have found that the chemical behaviour of elements is related to the electron arrangements of their atoms.

- Elements in the same Group of the Periodic Table have the same number of outer shell electrons and similar chemical properties.

- The three sub-atomic particles which make up almost all atoms have different properties.

Particle	Mass (amu)	Charge	Location
proton (p)	1	1+	nucleus
neutron (n)	1	0	nucleus
electron (e)	negligible (~1/1850)	1–	electron cloud

- The charge on the nucleus is positive due to the protons present.

- Since atoms are electrically neutral, they must contain the same number of positive and negative charges i.e. the same number of protons and electrons are present in an atom.

- Electron arrangements for atoms are found in Data Booklets and they may also appear below the chemical symbols for the elements in some Periodic Tables.

H 1							He 2
Li 2,1	Be 2,2	B 2,3	C 2,4	N 2,5	O 2,6	F 2,7	Ne 2,8
Na 2,8,1	Mg 2,8,2	Al 2,8,3	Si 2,8,4	P 2,8,5	S 2,8,6	Cl 2,8,7	Ar 2,8,8
K 2,8,8,1	Ca 2,8,8,2						

- Elements are arranged in the Periodic Table in order of atomic number, H = 1, He = 2, etc.

- The atomic number is often shown below, and to the left of, the element symbol e.g. as in $_1H$, $_3Li$, $_6C$, $_{17}Cl$, $_{20}Ca$, etc.

- The mass number of an atom is equal to the total number of protons plus neutrons in the nucleus of the atom.

- The mass number is shown above, and to the left of, the element symbol e.g. as in ^1H, ^7Li, ^{12}C, ^{35}Cl, ^{40}Ca, etc.

- Atoms represented by nuclide notation i.e. $^{12}_6C$ show mass number and atomic number.

- This notation is used to find the number of protons, electrons and neutrons in atoms.

- Mass number – atomic number = number of neutrons

- $^{12}_6C$ atoms have 6 p, 6 e and 6 n

  $^{35}_{17}Cl$ atoms have 17 p, 17 e and 18 n

  $^{24}_{12}Mg$ atoms have 12 p, 12 e and 12 n

- All atoms **except** ^1_1H contain neutrons as well as protons in their nuclei.

Isotopes

- It is quite common to find atoms of the same element with the same atomic number but different mass numbers e.g. $^{35}_{17}Cl$ and $^{37}_{17}Cl$.

- Chemists call such atoms isotopes and most elements are found as a mixture of isotopes.

- In fact, a machine called a mass spectrometer can measure the individual masses of atoms to reveal that most elements have isotopes.

- The difference in mass number is due to different numbers of neutrons present in the nuclei of the atoms.

You should be able to use the atomic number and mass number information supplied with the two isotopes of chlorine to understand the composition of each chlorine isotope.

$^{35}_{17}Cl$ atoms have 17 p, 17 e and 18 n

but,

$^{37}_{17}Cl$ atoms have 17 p, 17 e and 20 n

- Hydrogen is a mixture of three isotopes:

$^{1}_{1}H$ atoms have 1 p, 1 e and 0 n

$^{2}_{1}H$ atoms have 1 p, 1 e and 1 n

$^{3}_{1}H$ atoms have 1 p, 1 e and 2 n

- Mass numbers and atomic numbers are **always** whole numbers.

e.g. $^{20}_{10}Ne$ $^{22}_{10}Ne$ $^{35}_{17}Cl$ $^{37}_{17}Cl$

- Relative atomic masses for these elements are not, however, whole numbers! i.e. Ne = 20.2 and Cl = 35.5

- The relative atomic mass of an element is an 'average' mass of its atoms which takes into account the relative abundances of each isotope present.

- Neon has two isotopes:

$^{20}_{10}Ne$ (90 %) and $^{22}_{10}Ne$ (10 %), so the relative atomic mass of neon is found as follows:

$$\text{Relative atomic mass} = \frac{90}{100} \times 20 + \frac{10}{100} \times 22$$

$$= 18.0 + 2.2$$

$$= 20.2$$

- Chlorine has two isotopes:

$^{35}_{17}Cl$ (75 %) and $^{37}_{17}Cl$ (25 %), so the relative atomic mass of chlorine is found as follows:

$$\text{Relative atomic mass} = \frac{75}{100} \times 35 + \frac{25}{100} \times 37$$

$$= 26.25 + 9.25$$

$$= 35.5$$

(d) Bonding, structure and properties

Bonding

- Atoms bond with each other by either sharing outer electrons or by swapping outer electrons to achieve greater chemical stability.

- Chemical stability is achieved by the bonding atoms becoming like the Noble Gases in terms of their full outer shells of electrons.

- Noble gas atoms do not bond with each other to form molecules because the outer electron energy levels (or shells) are 'full'.

- Noble gases exist as single atoms held together by very weak bonds.

weak van der Waals' forces between atoms of noble gases

- In covalent bonding, non-metal atoms bond by sharing electron pairs – usually one electron is supplied by each atom – to form strongly bonded molecules.

molecules of elements (same atoms present)

molecules of compounds (different atoms present)

- The metals in Groups 1, 2 and 3 of the Periodic Table have atoms bonded by the electrostatic force of attraction between delocalised outer electrons and lattices of positively charged ions.

part of a metal lattice

- Some elements in Group 4 form large, strong, covalently bonded 'network molecules' or, in the case of the lower members of the Group, Sn and Pb, use the delocalised outer shell electrons to bond atoms as in metals.

part of a covalent network

- The atoms of non-metals in Groups 5, 6 and 7 can also bond covalently to form either elements, by sharing electron pairs between identical atoms, or compounds by sharing electron pairs between different atoms.

- In most covalent compounds, the electron pairs forming the bonds are **unequally** shared giving rise to polar-covalent molecules e.g. H_2O (water) molecules are polar (see later).

- Metal and non-metal atoms can bond together by creating oppositely charged ions through electron transfer from the metal atoms to the non-metal atoms.

- The electrostatic force of attraction between ions of opposite charge is called ionic bonding.

part of an ionic lattice

Structure - discrete molecules

- Molecules are groups of atoms held together by covalent bonds.

Ball model-making kits are essential at this stage to aid your learning about bonding in molecules.

- Hydrogen exists as a diatomic ('two atom') molecule held together by a covalent bond.

- Overlapping electron cloud pictures can show where the covalent bond is formed:

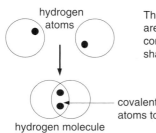

hydrogen atoms

The two hydrogen nuclei are held together by their common attraction for the shared pair of electrons.

covalent bond – the link holding the atoms together in the molecule.

hydrogen molecule

- From either a ball model of a hydrogen molecule, which would appear like ●—● or ●●, or a molecular picture, it is seen that the formula of hydrogen is H_2.

- The Group 7 elements ('Halogens') exist, like hydrogen, as diatomic molecules with a single covalent bond e.g. chlorine

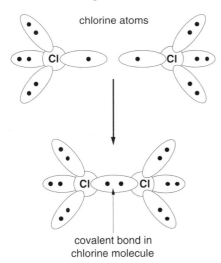

chlorine atoms

covalent bond in chlorine molecule

- From either a ball model of a chlorine molecule, which would appear like ⬤—⬤ or ⬤⬤, or a molecular picture, it is seen that the formula of chlorine is Cl_2.

- Similar diagrams can be drawn to show the diatomic molecular structures of F_2, Br_2, I_2.

- Diatomic molecules may be identified from their chemical formulae e.g. carbon monoxide, CO, and hydrogen chloride, HCl.

- It is possible for atoms of some non-metal elements to have more than one half-filled electron cloud leading to multiple covalent bonding within molecules.

- Atoms with six outer electrons have two half-filled electron pair clouds.

- Oxygen atoms join by overlapping their two half-filled electron clouds forming a double covalent bond.

ball model   O=O
                  structural
                  formula

- Oxygen is also a diatomic molecule with the formula O_2.

- Atoms with five outer electrons have three half-filled electron pair clouds.

- Nitrogen atoms join by overlapping their three half-filled electron clouds, forming a triple covalent bond.

ball model   N≡N
                  structural
                  formula

- The formula of nitrogen is N_2.

- Hydrogen, oxygen, nitrogen, fluorine and chlorine exist as gaseous diatomic molecules at normal temperature.

Weak van der Waals' forces act **between** molecules to hold them together. They are **much weaker** than the covalent bonds within the molecules.

- Atoms of different non-metals can also share half-filled electron clouds to form stable, covalently bonded, compound molecules where the number of half-filled electron clouds available for bonding determines both the formula and the shape of the molecule.

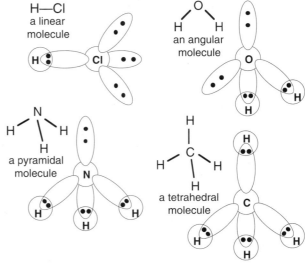

H—Cl
a linear molecule

an angular molecule

a pyramidal molecule

a tetrahedral molecule

- The formulae for each of these discrete molecules give the actual numbers of atoms in each molecule i.e. HCl (2 atoms), H_2O (3 atoms), NH_3 (4 atoms) and CH_4 (5 atoms).

Structure - covalent network lattices

- The atoms of some elements in Group 4 of the Periodic Table are bonded in covalent networks i.e. large lattice structures of covalently bonded atoms.

- Carbon exists as two high melting point covalent network solids – diamond and graphite.

diamond

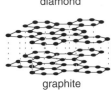
graphite

There is a regular tetrahedral arrangement of covalently bonded carbon atoms within the diamond network structure. All four outer electrons of each carbon atom are involved in strong covalent bonding. The layered structure of graphite has covalently bonded carbon atoms arranged in hexagonal plates. Three of the four outer electrons of each carbon atom are involved in strong covalent bonding within the hexagonal layers. The fourth outer electron on each carbon atom is free to move within the hexagonal layers. These electron movements within layers create weak van der Waals' forces between the layers in the graphite lattice.

- Silicon, another of the Group 4 elements, has a strongly bonded, covalent network structure similar to that of diamond.

- Silicon carbide, SiC, forms a covalent network molecule with a diamond-type lattice structure which is very difficult to break down since this involves overcoming extremely strong covalent bonds.

- Within this giant covalent network structure, each silicon atom is bonded to four carbon atoms, and each carbon atom is bonded to four silicon atoms.

- The formula for a covalent network compound is the simplest ratio of atoms e.g. Si:C = 1:1 in silicon carbide, hence the formula is SiC.

Structure - ionic lattices

- Metal atoms cannot achieve a stable electron arrangement by sharing electrons with other atoms to form molecules.

- In reactions with non-metal atoms, metal atoms gain stability by losing their outer shell electrons to form stable, positively charged ions.

e.g. Li atoms
electron arrangement 2, 1
during reaction lose 1e⁻

Li^+ A lithium ion
2 ⊕

e.g. Al atoms
electron arrangement 2, 8, 3
during reaction lose 3e⁻

Al^{3+} An aluminium ion
2, 8 (3+)

- In reactions, these 'lost' electrons from metal atoms are gained by non-metal atoms to form stable ions which are negatively charged.

e.g. F atoms
electron arrangement 2, 7
during reaction gain 1e⁻

F^- A fluoride ion
2, 8 ⊖

e.g. S atoms
electron arrangement 2, 8, 6
during reaction gain 2e⁻

S^{2-} A sulphide ion
2, 8, 8 (2-)

- In the reaction between the metal sodium and the non-metal chlorine, there is a transfer of electrons between atoms resulting in the formation of oppositely charged ions.

Reacting elements	Na	Cl
Electron arrangements	2, 8, 1	2, 8, 7
During reaction	loses 1e⁻	gains 1e⁻
	transfer of an electron	
Resulting in the electron arrangements	2, 8	2, 8, 8
Formation of ions	Na⁺	Cl⁻

There is electrostatic attraction between the oppositely charged ions called ionic bonding.

Na^+Cl^-

- Ionic compounds are made up of positively charged metal ions and negatively charged non-metal ions arranged in giant, three-dimensional, cube-shaped lattices at normal temperatures.

- The formula for an ionic compound is the simplest ratio of positive ions : negative ions i.e. in NaCl and CaO the ratio is 1:1 but in $CaCl_2$ it is 1:2 and in $(NH_4)_2SO_4$ it is 2:1.

Structure - metallic lattices

- Most elements are metals, occurring mainly in Groups 1, 2 and 3 but also as the Transition Metals found between Groups 2 and 3.

- The outer electron(s) of each atom can move freely within a giant lattice of positive ions.

- The force of attraction between a lattice of positively charged ions and mobile, delocalised, outer electrons is called metallic bonding.

fast-moving outer shell electrons

part of a metallic lattice

Properties

Conductivity

- Metallic elements conduct electricity when solid and when molten, as the delocalised electrons can move under an applied voltage.

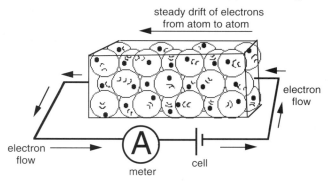

steady drift of electrons from atom to atom

electron flow

electron flow

meter cell

- Carbon (graphite) can be made to conduct electricity due to the freely moving electrons within its layered structure.

- Mercury (Hg), the only liquid metal at normal temperature, is a very good conductor.

- Metals (and graphite) are not changed chemically while conducting electricity.

- Covalent solids, liquids and solutions i.e. those substances made of molecules, are insulators or non-conductors of electricity.

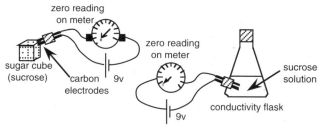

zero reading on meter

zero reading on meter

sugar cube (sucrose) carbon electrodes 9v

sucrose solution

conductivity flask 9v

- In solid ionic compounds, the ions are 'locked' together in the giant lattice and are not free to move about to conduct electricity.

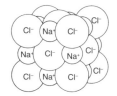

Molten ionic compounds, and aqueous solutions of those soluble ionic solids, are good conductors of electricity as the ions can now move around freely.

Melting points and boiling points

- Melting points and boiling points of metals are fairly high (except Group 1 'Alkali Metals') due to the strength of metallic bonding holding the giant lattices together.

e.g.

metal	m.p. / °C	b.p. / °C
Cu	1083	2567
Fe	1535	2750
Ag	962	2212
Na	98	883

- Substances with covalent network structures have high melting points and boiling points due to the presence of strong covalent bonds.

e.g.

substance	m.p. / °C	b.p. / °C
C	3550	4827
Si	1410	2355
SiO_2	1610	–

- Ionic compounds have high melting points and boiling points because strong ionic bonds have to be broken to bring about the changes of state.

e.g.

substance	m.p. / °C	b.p. / °C
NaCl	808	1517
KBr	734	1384
$MgCl_2$	714	1416

- Substances which exist as discrete covalent molecules have low melting points and low boiling points since very weak forces are being broken to change the states.

e.g.

substance	m.p. / °C	b.p. / °C
H_2	– 259	– 252
N_2	– 210	– 196
Cl_2	– 101	– 35
CCl_4	– 23	77

Solubility

- Water is a polar molecule and because of its bonding and structure, it is a good solvent for most ionic compounds. Most metals are insoluble in water and other solvents.

Oxygen has a greater share of bonded electrons (gets a slight –ve charge) than hydrogen atoms (get a slight +ve charge). The slight charges on H_2O molecules (polar covalent) are attracted to, and are able to bond to, ions of the opposite charge in ionic solids.

∂+ means 'slightly positive'

Note: The highly polar nature of H_2O results in hydrogen bonding which accounts for some very unusual properties. It boils at 100 °C, very high for its small molecular mass, and when solid, it floats - rather than sinks - in its own liquid!

- Ionic compounds are usually soluble in other polar solvents e.g. ethanol, but insoluble in non-polar solvents such as petrol and CH_3CCl_3.

- Covalent solids which are not soluble in water e.g. $I_2(s)$, may dissolve in non-polar solvents much more readily.

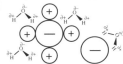

part of an ionic lattice 'being dissolved' by H_2O

these ions are now 'in solution'

insoluble in water

soluble in nor

Electrolysis

- Electricity passing through metal wires is a flow of electrons causing no chemical change.

- Melts (molten ionic compounds) or solutions of ionic compounds can conduct electricity because positively and negatively charged ions can move through these electrolytes.

- Direct current (d.c.) passed through melts or aqueous solutions of ionic compounds causes chemical change, especially decomposition, at the electrodes. This is called electrolysis.

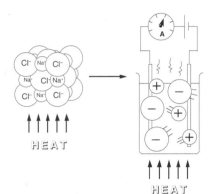

Melting has released ions from the lattice to move about and conduct electricity. Positive ions migrate towards the negative electrode and negative ions migrate towards the positive electrode.

- During electrolysis of the molten sodium chloride, positively charged sodium ions move towards the negative electrode (cathode) where electrons are gained:

$$2Na^+(l) + 2e^- \longrightarrow 2Na(l)$$
ions $\qquad\qquad$ atoms

- Negatively charged chloride ions move towards the positive electrode (anode) where electrons are lost:

$$2Cl^-(l) \longrightarrow Cl_2(g) + 2e^-$$
ions $\qquad\qquad$ molecules

Overall, $2NaCl(l) \longrightarrow 2Na(l) + Cl_2(g)$

- Evidence for ion movement and subsequent electrolysis may be obtained from coloured ion migration experiments.

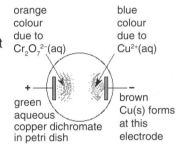

orange colour due to $Cr_2O_7^{2-}(aq)$

blue colour due to $Cu^{2+}(aq)$

green aqueous copper dichromate in petri dish

brown Cu(s) forms at this electrode

(e) Chemical symbolism

Formulae: prefixes

- Some help in writing correct formulae is often given by prefixes e.g. mono (one), di (two), tri (three), tetra (four), penta (five), hexa (six).

- Carbon monoxide is CO, carbon dioxide is CO_2, carbon tetrachloride is CCl_4, phosphorus trichloride is PCl_3, phosphorus pentachloride is PCl_5 and xenon hexafluoride is XeF_6.

Formulae: using the data booklet

- Here is a way, using valencies, to work out chemical formulae for any two element compounds with names ending in '–ide'. (Remember: hydroxides are an exception!)

- Write down the symbols of the elements in the compound and put the valencies above them:
  e.g. $\quad$ 4 $\quad$ 1
  $\qquad$ C $\quad$ H
  Now 'cross over' the valencies:
  i.e. $\quad$ 4 $\quad$ 1

  to give $C_1 \quad H_4$

  It is not necessary to write a ' $_1$ ' in a chemical formula, and so the formula of the simplest compound formed between the elements carbon and hydrogen, carbon hydride or hydrogen carbide, is written as CH_4.

- 'Cancel' the valencies down, if required, to a smaller whole number ratio i.e. 2:2 would become 1:1 as in ZnS (valency Zn = 2; S = 2).

Formulae: compounds and group ions

- Group ions (or complex ions) appear in the Data Booklet with the numerical value of the charge being its valency e.g. the ion NH_4^+ has a valency = 1.

- Ions placed 'side-by-side' must be balanced for the charges present.
  e.g. NH_4^+ and NO_3^- would be present in a 1:1 ratio in ammonium nitrate, formula $NH_4^+NO_3^-$. Without charges, the formula is NH_4NO_3 .

- Sodium sulphate has the formula Na_2SO_4, i.e. the correct 2:1 ratio of $Na^+:SO_4^{2-}$ ions.

Formulae: Roman numerals

- Some elements, particularly Transition Metals, can have more than one valency!

- The valency is written in Roman numerals, in brackets, after the name of the element.
  e.g. copper(I) oxide has copper valency = 1, and iron(III) sulphate has iron valency = 3.

- Manganese(II) oxide is MnO (oxide ion is O^{2-}); while manganese(IV) oxide is MnO_2.

Formulae: brackets and some group ions

- Ammonium phosphate, containing both NH_4^+ and PO_4^{3-} ions, must use brackets placed around the ammonium ion in the formula for the compound i.e. $(NH_4^+)_3PO_4^{3-}$ – showing ion charges – or, $(NH_4)_3PO_4$ without ion charges.

- Magnesium hydroxide, containing Mg^{2+} ions and OH^- ions, must be shown as $Mg^{2+}(OH^-)_2$ or $Mg(OH)_2$, and **not** as $MgOH_2$.

(f) The mole

Number of moles

- The relative formula mass of a substance is the sum of the relative atomic masses of all the atoms in the chemical formula.

Example:

Calculate the formula mass of potassium carbonate.

Write the correct formula: K_2CO_3

Look up the Data Booklet for the individual relative atomic masses:
$$K = 39; C = 12; O = 16$$

Relative formula mass $= (2 \times 39) + 12 + (3 \times 16)$
$$= 78 + 12 + 48$$
$$= 138$$

Relative formula mass of $K_2CO_3 = 138$

- The mole is an international term used by chemists for a certain quantity of a chemical substance.

- At Intermediate 2, one mole (mol for short) of a chemical substance is the relative formula mass in grams, or the gram formula mass.

It is quite a simple idea at this stage of your chemistry and a few examples should help you to accept this usage of the chemical mole (mol).

- Calculate the mass of one mole (1 mol) of carbon hydride.

Write the correct formula: CH_4

Look up the Data Booklet for the individual relative atomic masses:
$$C = 12; H = 1$$

Relative formula mass $= 12 + (4 \times 1)$
$$= 12 + 4$$
$$= 16$$

Relative formula mass of $CH_4 = 16$

Gram formula mass of $CH_4 = 16$ g

One mole (1 mol) of CH_4 weighs 16 g.

- Calculate the mass of two moles (2 mol) of the compound with the formula $Mg(NO_3)_2$.

$Mg(NO_3)_2$ is the formula of magnesium nitrate.

Looking up the Data Booklet for the individual relative atomic masses gives:
$$Mg = 24; N = 14; O = 16$$

Relative formula mass $= 24 + 2 [14 + (3 \times 16)]$
$$= 24 + 2 [62]$$
$$= 148$$

Relative formula mass of $Mg(NO_3)_2 = 148$

Gram formula mass of $Mg(NO_3)_2 = 148$ g $= 1$ mol

Two moles (2 mol) of $Mg(NO_3)_2$ weighs 296 g.

Masses to moles and moles to masses

You must be able to handle the interchange of masses and moles with some confidence!

$$moles = \frac{mass\ of\ substance}{gram\ formula\ mass}$$

$$mass\ of\ substance = moles \times gram\ formula\ mass$$

- How many moles of water are present in 54 g of the liquid?

Write the correct formula: H_2O

Calculate the relative formula mass.
Relative formula mass of $H_2O = 2 + 16 = 18$
The mass of 1 mole of $H_2O = 18$ g

$$Moles\ of\ H_2O = \frac{54\ g}{18\ g} = 3\ moles\ (3\ mol)$$

- What is the mass of 0.1 mol sodium chloride?

Write the correct formula: NaCl

Calculate the relative formula mass.
Relative formula mass of NaCl $= 23 + 35.5 = 58.5$

State that the mass of 1 mol NaCl $= 58.5$ g

$$Mass\ of\ NaCl = 0.1 \times 58.5\ g = 5.85\ g$$

Using balanced equations

Remember, as soon as you have the balanced equation, you have the ratio of the moles of both reactants and products! The masses of either reactants or products can now be calculated from the moles!

- Study the balanced equation and the kind of information which may be calculated from it:

2Ca	+	O_2	→	2CaO

	2Ca	O_2	2CaO
=>	2 mol	1 mol	2 mol
=>	80 g	32 g	112 g
=>	1 mol	0.5 mol	1 mol
=>	40 g	16 g	56 g
=>	0.5 mol	0.25 mol	0.5 mol
=>	20 g	8 g	28 g

- Study the balanced equation and the kind of information which may be calculated from it:

N_2	+	$3H_2$	→	$2NH_3$

	N_2	$3H_2$	$2NH_3$
=>	1 mol	3 mol	2 mol
=>	28 g	6 g	34 g
=>	2 mol	6 mol	4 mol
=>	56 g	12 g	68 g
=>	0.5 mol	1.5 mol	1 mol
=>	14 g	3 g	17 g

Unit 2 · Carbon Compounds   Intermediate 2

(a) Fuels
Combustion

- From the earliest times, combustion (burning) of fuels has been used for cooking, heating and lighting.

- When fuels burn, they react with O_2 to release energy mainly as heat (and some light).

- Modern societies make even greater use of fuels for these purposes and a lot more!

Fossil fuels

- The main fuels presently in use are the fossil fuels – coal, oil and natural gas.

- Coal formed over many millions of years from the decaying remains of mainly plant material.

- Many of these plants were fern-like but some were as big as trees.

semi-tropical vegetation and swamp plants → hard black solid, mainly carbon

- Crude oil and natural gas formed under the earth's surface from the decaying bodies of tiny sea organisms over many millions of years. They are found in sedimentary rocks.

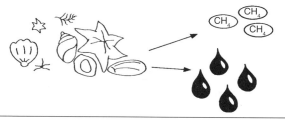

- If fossil fuels are used up too quickly, this could lead to a fuel crisis in the next century!

- The Earth is the only source of all our fuels. They are finite resources i.e. they are limited in supply and cannot be replaced!

- Most forms of transport will be affected badly by a shortage of fuels!

- Generation of electricity will be a huge problem since coal and oil are burned up in huge amounts by power stations!

- Most of our modern plastics, fibres, paints, dyes, drugs, medicines, etc, are made from the raw materials obtained from coal, crude oil and natural gas!

- The need for coke (from coal) in steel-making may threaten the closure of this already dwindling UK industry!

Some burning issues

- Oil and natural gas are mainly composed of hydrocarbons which are covalent substances containing only H and C bonded atoms.

- Hydrocarbons burn completely in a plentiful supply of air forming carbon dioxide and water as the only products.

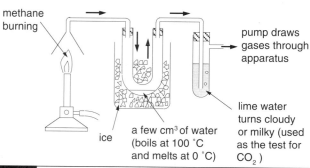

methane burning / pump draws gases through apparatus / lime water turns cloudy or milky (used as the test for CO_2) / ice / a few cm^3 of water (boils at 100 °C and melts at 0 °C)

- Hydrocarbons burn incompletely in a limited supply of O_2 to also produce carbon monoxide (an extremely poisonous gas) and soot (C).

- Soot particles are also a serious pollutant from the incomplete combustion of diesel fuel.

- Lead, unburnt hydrocarbons, CO and NO_x (from the sparking of N_2 and O_2 in air) are emitted from cars with leaded-petrol engines.

- Leaded-petrol will be banned from general sale from 1st January, 2000!

- Catalytic converters fitted to most car exhaust systems convert the poisonous gases NO_x and CO to the harmless gases N_2 and CO_2.

- Coals and oils may have sulphur compounds present which burn to produce the toxic gas SO_2 which contributes to 'acid rain' in the air.

Fractional distillation

- Crude oil is a complex mixture of many chemical compounds, mainly hydrocarbons.

Your teacher will probably not have performed a fractional distillation experiment in the laboratory using 'real' crude oil because it is a very harmful substance. It is more sensible to use a mixture of less harmful oils to simulate a crude oil. This can be separated because, like the crude oil, its components have different boiling point ranges.

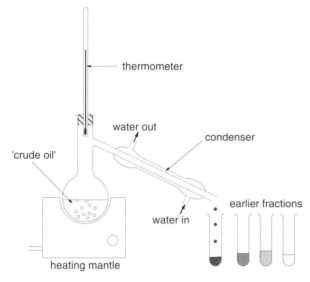

- Early fractions boil off at low temperatures and are almost colourless. Later fractions boil off at higher temperatures and are coloured yellow, then go eventually green/brown.

- Early fractions are quite 'runny' (less viscous) but later fractions become very thick (more viscous) and eventually they have difficulty running out of the condenser.

- On testing, early fractions evaporate more quickly than later fractions and they are also easier to ignite.

- Differences in the properties of hydrocarbon fractions i.e. boiling point, viscosity, ease of evaporation and flammability (or ease of ignition) are due to differences in the sizes of molecules in the fractions.

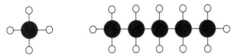

- As molecular size ↑, boiling point ↑

- As molecular size ↑, viscosity ↑

- As molecular size ↑, ease of evaporation ↓

- As molecular size ↑, flammability ↓

- Oil refineries separate and purify the many different hydrocarbons found in crude oil by a process called fractional distillation.

- Separation of the mixture of hydrocarbons is achieved because of the differences in boiling points of the hydrocarbons present.

- Separation takes place in a tall, heated tower called a fractionating column where the various oil fractions are collected at different levels from pipes on the side of the tower.

- Each fraction contains a new mixture of hydrocarbons within a boiling point range.

- The first fraction contains hydrocarbon gases with the lowest boiling point range. They will leave from the top of the fractionating tower.

- The last fraction contains hydrocarbon solids with the highest boiling point range. They are found in the residue at the foot of the tower.

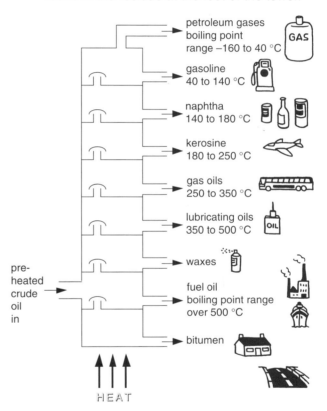

- Petroleum gases have C_1 to C_4 molecules.

- Gasoline/naphtha have C_5 to C_{10} molecules.

- Bitumen molecules are C_{25} and higher!

- The strength of the van der Waals' forces between hydrocarbon molecules increases as the size of these molecules in the fractions increases.

(b) Nomenclature and structural formulae

The IUPAC convention for systematic naming will be used with molecules of alkanes, alkenes, cycloalkanes, alkanols, alkanoic acids and esters. You should know how to write molecular formulae and structural formulae - both full and shortened - for many of these compounds.

Hydrocarbons

Alkanes

- Alkanes (names end in '–ane') are a subset of the set of hydrocarbons.

- The first three alkanes are methane, ethane and propane with molecular formulae CH_4, C_2H_6 and C_3H_8, respectively.

- Full structural formulae of these alkanes are shown by:

methane   ethane   propane

- Shortened structural formulae are used to show how atoms are grouped together within molecules without drawing all the covalent bond 'lines'.

  e.g. CH_3CH_3 $CH_3CH_2CH_3$
           ethane   propane

Branched-chain alkanes

- Carbon atoms in alkanes can bond to the main continuous carbon chain as 'side-chains' to form branched-chain alkanes.

- The 'parent' name is decided by the longest chain of carbon atoms which are numbered to indicate the position of alkyl groups which may be $-CH_3$ (methyl), $-C_2H_5$ (ethyl), etc.

Remember to use lower numbers where possible to indicate the position of 'branched' alkyl groups. e.g.

2-methylpropane   2-methylbutane   2-methylpentane
                    (not 3-methylbutane) (not 4-methylpentane)

$CH_3CH(CH_3)CH_3$ $CH_3CH(CH_3)CH_2CH_3$ $CH_3CH(CH_3)CH_2CH_2CH_3$

| C_4H_{10} | C_5H_{12} | C_6H_{14} |

Alkenes

- Alkenes (contain a C=C bond in molecules and have names ending in '–ene') are a subset of the set of hydrocarbons.

- The C=C position is indicated in the name of the larger, straight-chain alkene molecules.

- Ethene, propene and butene have molecular formulae C_2H_4, C_3H_6 and C_4H_8, respectively.

- Alkane molecules which have a continuous, single line, or chain, of bonded carbon atoms are called *straight-chain alkanes*.

- The next five straight-chain alkanes are called butane, pentane, hexane, heptane and octane where the name prefixes refer to the number of carbon atoms in the straight-chain.

Meth	= 1 'carbon atom'
Eth	= 2 'carbon atoms'
Prop	= 3 'carbon atoms'
But	= 4 'carbon atoms'
Pent	= 5 'carbon atoms'
Hex	= 6 'carbon atoms'
Hept	= 7 'carbon atoms'
Oct	= 8 'carbon atoms'

You should be able to name all C_1 to C_8 straight-chain alkanes from their molecular formulae and also from their structural formulae - either the full or the shortened version.

- Butane has the molecular formula C_4H_{10} and shortened structural formula $CH_3CH_2CH_2CH_3$.

- C_5H_{12} is pentane which has the following full structural formula:

- Hexane, C_6H_{14}, heptane, C_7H_{16} and octane, C_8H_{18}, exist as liquids at normal temperatures.

Can you see that heptane will have the shortened structural formula $CH_3CH_2CH_2CH_2CH_2CH_2CH_3$?

- The positions of more than one 'branched' alkyl group are indicated in the following way:

2,2-dimethylpropane   3,4-dimethylhexane

$CH_3C(CH_3)_2CH_3$ $CH_3CH_2CH(CH_3)CH(CH_3)CH_2CH_3$

| C_5H_{12} | | C_8H_{18} |

You should practise systematic naming and drawing full and shortened structural formulae for all of the branched-chain alkanes from molecule size C_4 up to C_8!

2,4-dimethylhexane
(not 3,5-dimethylhexane)

| C_8H_{18} |

Have you spotted different alkanes with the same molecular formula?

ethene
$CH_2=CH_2$

| C_2H_4 |

but-1-ene
$CH_2=CHCH_2CH_3$

| C_4H_8 |

but-2-ene
$CH_3CH=CHCH_3$

| C_4H_8 |

propene
$CH_2=CHCH_3$

| C_3H_6 |

Practise systematic naming and drawing formulae for alkenes with up to C_8 atoms per molecule!

Cycloalkanes

- This subset of the hydrocarbons have names starting with 'cyclo–' and ending in '–ane'.

- The 'cyclo–' refers to the ring of carbon atoms in each molecule held together by single covalent C – C bonds.

- The first cycloalkane is cyclopropane, C_3H_6.

- The structural formulae of cyclopropane are shown here:

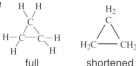

full   shortened

- Cyclobutane has the molecular formula C_4H_8 and structural formulae as shown below:

```
  H  H
  |  |
H-C--C-H          H₂C────CH₂
  |  |     full    |      |      shortened
H-C--C-H          H₂C────CH₂
  |  |
  H  H
```

- Both cyclopropane and cyclobutane are rather unstable hydrocarbons and the easiest cycloalkanes to obtain are the more stable 5– and 6–membered ring compounds.

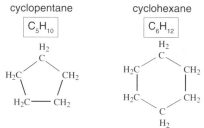

shortened structural formulae

You should be able to write the names, molecular formulae and structural formulae of cycloalkanes from C_3 to C_8 atoms per molecule.

- The general formula for cycloalkanes is C_nH_{2n}, the same as that for the alkenes.

Isomers

- When compounds have the same molecular formula but different structural formulae, they are called *isomers* and exhibit *isomerism*.

- Alkanes first exhibit isomerism with the two hydrocarbons of formula C_4H_{10}.

```
  H  H  H  H              H  CH₃ H
  |  |  |  |              |   |  |
H-C--C--C--C-H          H-C---C--C-H
  |  |  |  |              |   |  |
  H  H  H  H              H   H  H
    butane              2-methylpropane
```

- Pentane, C_5H_{12}, has three isomers:

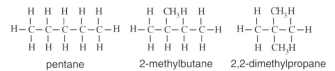

pentane   2-methylbutane   2,2-dimethylpropane

- Straight-chain alkenes also exhibit isomerism.

```
H          H  H                H  H             H  H  H  H
 \         |  |                |  |             |  |  |  |
  C=C--C--CH₃          H-C----C-H          H-C--C=C--C-H
 /                              |  |             |        |
H  H                    H-C----C-H             H        H
                          |  |
but-1-ene                 H  H              but-2-ene
                        cyclobutane
```

- Alkenes are isomeric with cycloalkanes.

Structural formulae can be written with covalent bonds in different directions, so always look closely before you decide if molecules are isomers!

The molecules opposite are both propane molecules!

They are not isomers!

```
  H   H   H
  |   |   |
H-C---C---C-H
  |   |   |
  H   H   H


        H
        |
      H-C-H
  H   |
  |   |
H-C---C-H
  |   |
  H   H
```

Alkanols

- Alkanols are characterised by the –OH group in molecules and have names ending in '–ol'.

- Alkanols have the general formula $C_nH_{2n+1}OH$ and are named according to the IUPAC system.

You should be able to relate to names, molecular and structural formulae of C_1 to C_8 straight-chain alkanols.

```
  H              H  H          H  H  H           H  OH H
  |              |  |          |  |  |           |  |  |
H-C-OH         H-C--C-OH     H-C--C--C-OH      H-C--C--C-H
  |              |  |          |  |  |           |  |  |
  H              H  H          H  H  H           H  H  H
methanol       ethanol       propan-1-ol        propan-2-ol
```

CH_3OH CH_3CH_2OH $CH_3CH_2CH_2OH$ $CH_3CH(OH)CH_3$

$\boxed{CH_4O}$ $\boxed{C_2H_6O}$ $\boxed{C_3H_8O}$ $\boxed{C_3H_8O}$

Can you see why isomerism is just not possible with either methanol or ethanol?

- Propan-1-ol and propan-2-ol **are** isomers.

- As the carbon chain in alkanols increases in length, the position of the –OH group must be correctly stated in the systematic names.

```
  H  H  H  H
  |  |  |  |
H-C--C--C--C-OH
  |  |  |  |
  H  H  H  H
CH₃CH₂CH₂CH₂OH
```
$\boxed{C_4H_{10}O}$

This is **butan-1-ol**.

It is not butan-4-ol!

This is **butan-2-ol**.

It is not butan-3-ol!

```
  H  H  H  H
  |  |  |  |
H-C--C--C--C-H
  |  |  |  |
  H  H  OH H
CH₃CH₂CH(OH)CH₃
```
$\boxed{C_4H_{10}O}$

```
  H  H  H  H  H  H
  |  |  |  |  |  |
H-C--C--C--C--C--C-H
  |  |  |  |  |  |
  H  H  OH H  H  H
CH₃CH₂CH(OH)CH₂CH₂CH₃
```
$\boxed{C_6H_{14}O}$

This is **hexan-3-ol**.

It is not hexan-4-ol!

Alkanoic acids

- Alkanoic acids are characterised by a –COOH group (carboxyl group) in molecules and have the parent names ending in ' –oic'.

You should be able to relate to names, molecular and structural formulae (full and shortened) of C_1 to C_8 straight-chain alkanoic acids.

- Methanoic acid is the simplest alkanoic acid.

You may see the full structural formula displayed in two different ways:

methanoic acid
HCOOH $\boxed{CH_2O_2}$

- Ethanoic acid is probably the best known member of the alkanoic acids.

ethanoic acid
CH_3COOH $\boxed{C_2H_4O_2}$

- Other straight-chain alkanoic acids include:

propanoic acid	CH_3CH_2COOH
butanoic acid	$CH_3CH_2CH_2COOH$
pentanoic acid	$CH_3CH_2CH_2CH_2COOH$
hexanoic acid	$CH_3CH_2CH_2CH_2CH_2COOH$

Can you name the next two alkanoic acids with the molecular formulae $C_7H_{14}O_2$ and $C_8H_{16}O_2$?

Esters

You should be able to relate to names (all esters end in '–oate'), molecular and structural formulae and to the products of the breakdown of esters.

- The characteristic ester group (–COO–) has oxygen atoms from both the parent alkanol and alkanoic acid molecules.

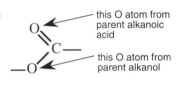
this O atom from parent alkanoic acid
this O atom from parent alkanol

Alkanol	Alkanoic acid	Ester name	Structural formula (shortened)
ethanol	ethanoic	ethyl ethanoate	$C_2H_5OOCCH_3$
methanol	propanoic	methyl propanoate	$CH_3OOCC_2H_5$
methanol	methanoic	methyl methanoate	CH_3OOCH

Note that the shortened structural formula of these esters may sometimes be given as:

$CH_3COOC_2H_5$	$C_2H_5COOCH_3$	$HCOOCH_3$
ethyl ethanoate	methyl propanoate	methyl methanoate

It is advisable to draw a full structural formula before attempting to identify an ester or to name an ester from a shortened structural formula.

- This is the full structural formula for the ester ethyl propanoate (**not** propyl ethanoate):

$CH_3CH_2OOCCH_2CH_3$ $\boxed{C_5H_{10}O_2}$

- Breakdown of this ester will give the alkanol, ethanol, C_2H_5OH, and the alkanoic acid, propanoic acid, CH_3CH_2COOH, as products.

Which straight-chain alkanoic acid is an isomer of this ester?

- This is the full structural formula for the ester methyl butanoate (**not** butyl methanoate):

$CH_3CH_2CH_2COOCH_3$ $\boxed{C_5H_{10}O_2}$

- Breakdown of this ester will give methanol, CH_3OH, and butanoic acid, $CH_3CH_2CH_2COOH$, as products.

Test yourself!

Identify these compounds (answers below):

A
$H-C=C-H$ (with H, H above)

B
$CH_3CH_2CH(OH)CH_3$

C
$H-C-C-C-C-C-H$ (pentan, OH on middle)

D
$CH_3COOC_2H_5$

E
$C=C-CH_3$ (with H, H, H)

F
C_4H_9COOH

G
$H-C-C-C-H$ (with OH)

H
$H-C-C=C-C-H$

I
C_3H_8

J
C_2H_5OH

Answers:
A is ethene; B is butan-2-ol; C is pentan-3-ol; D is ethyl ethanoate; E is propene; F is pentanoic acid; G is propan-2-ol; H is but-2-ene; I is propane; J is ethanol. Earlier, heptanoic and octanoic acids are the next in the series and pentanoic acid is isomeric with the ester ethyl propanoate.

(c) Reactions of carbon compounds

Addition reactions

- Alkenes are unsaturated hydrocarbons due to the presence of C=C bonds in their molecules which makes them more chemically reactive than either alkanes or cycloalkanes.

- Alkanes and cycloalkanes have only C–C bonds present in their molecules and are said to be saturated.

- Bromine solution (brown) decolourises very quickly on reaction with alkenes and this is used as a chemical test to distinguish between saturated and unsaturated hydrocarbons.

- Alkenes are very reactive hydrocarbons and can undergo addition reactions with diatomic molecules to form saturated products.

- Alkanes and cycloalkanes do not undergo addition reactions.

Some addition reactions of ethene

e.g. with bromine:

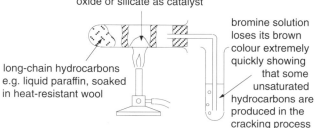

$$H-\underset{\underset{\text{ethene}}{\text{(unsaturated)}}}{\overset{\overset{H\quad H}{|\quad |}}{C=C}}-H \quad + \quad \underset{\text{bromine}}{Br_2} \longrightarrow \quad H-\underset{\underset{\text{1,2-dibromoethane}}{\underset{\text{(saturated)}}{Br\ \ Br}}}{\overset{\overset{H\quad H}{|\quad |}}{C-C}}-H$$

Can you see why the product has this name?

and, with hydrogen:

$$H-\underset{\underset{\text{ethene}}{\text{(unsaturated)}}}{\overset{\overset{H\quad H}{|\quad |}}{C=C}}-H \quad + \quad \underset{\text{hydrogen}}{H_2} \longrightarrow \quad H-\underset{\underset{\underset{\text{(saturated)}}{\text{ethane}}}{H\quad H}}{\overset{\overset{H\quad H}{|\quad |}}{C-C}}-H$$

and, with water:

$$H-\underset{\underset{\text{ethene}}{\text{(unsaturated)}}}{\overset{\overset{H\quad H}{|\quad |}}{C=C}}-H \quad + \quad \underset{\text{water}}{H_2O} \longrightarrow \quad H-\underset{\underset{\underset{\text{(saturated)}}{\text{ethanol}}}{H\quad H}}{\overset{\overset{H\quad H}{|\quad |}}{C-C}}-OH$$

Cracking

- The fractional distillation of crude oils produces huge quantities of long-chain hydrocarbons that the chemical industries cannot use.

  □ supply of long-chain hydrocarbons
  ■ amounts required by industries

- There is a much greater demand for smaller, more useful hydrocarbon molecules (e.g. gas, petrol and diesel) and so larger molecules in the higher boiling point range fractions are broken down in a chemical process called cracking.

- Cracking takes place at a lower temperature if a catalyst is used i.e. catalytic cracking.

- Catalytic cracking can be simulated in the laboratory.

Catalytic cracking in the laboratory

powdered aluminium oxide or silicate as catalyst

long-chain hydrocarbons e.g. liquid paraffin, soaked in heat-resistant wool

bromine solution loses its brown colour extremely quickly showing that some unsaturated hydrocarbons are produced in the cracking process

- The mixtures of saturated hydrocarbons (alkanes) and unsaturated hydrocarbons (alkenes) produced from catalytic cracking are due to the breaking of different bonds in the various hydrocarbon molecules.

  e.g. $\underset{\text{decane}}{C_{10}H_{22}} \longrightarrow \underset{\text{butane}}{C_4H_{10}} \quad + \quad \underset{\text{hexene}}{C_6H_{12}}$

  $\underset{\text{}}{C_{20}H_{42}} \longrightarrow \underset{\text{octane}}{2C_8H_{18}} \quad + \quad \underset{\text{propene}}{C_3H_6} \quad + \quad \underset{\text{carbon}}{C}$

- Industrial catalysts need to be regenerated i.e. by burning off the surface carbon (soot) which tends to poison the catalyst surface.

Ethanol - in alcoholic beverages

- Alcoholic drinks can be made by fermenting fruits or vegetables containing carbohydrates.

  e.g.

wine

barley

Best Malt 40%

whisky

grapes

- An enzyme in yeast acts as a catalyst in the fermentation process which breaks down glucose to form ethanol and carbon dioxide:

  $C_6H_{12}O_6 \longrightarrow 2C_2H_5OH + 2CO_2$

- The amount of ethanol produced during fermentation is not limitless since the enzyme is 'poisoned' at >15% alcohol.

- Distillation increases the concentration of ethanol (b.p. 80 °C) in the making of 'spirits'.

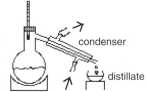

condenser

distillate

- Alcohol is a drug.

- Consuming alcohol in excess impairs the mind in the short term and is likely to have a damaging effect on health in the long term.

Ethanol - a chemical in great demand

- To meet market demand for this important alcohol, ethanol is made by methods other than the fermentation of carbohydrates.

- Industrial ethanol is manufactured by the catalytic hydration of ethene with steam.

$$CH_2 = CH_2 + H_2O \xrightarrow[\substack{\text{under high}\\\text{pressure}}]{\substack{H_3PO_4 \text{ on } SiO_2\\\text{at 300 °C}}} CH_3CH_2OH$$

- Dehydration of ethanol produces ethene.

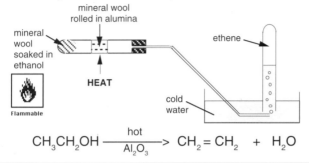

mineral wool rolled in alumina

mineral wool soaked in ethanol

HEAT

Flammable

ethene

cold water

$$CH_3CH_2OH \xrightarrow[Al_2O_3]{\text{hot}} CH_2 = CH_2 + H_2O$$

- In countries which can produce sugar cane on a very large scale and fairly economically, they have a renewable source of energy which can provide vast supplies of ethanol, C_2H_5OH, by fermentation processes.

- This ethanol is then used for blending with the more conventional car engine fuels i.e. petrols.

- Ethanol and other fuels with oxygen in their molecules are called *oxygenates* which, when added to petrols, increases their octane number to produce better fuels which result in less pollution from car exhausts.

- Ethanol burns very cleanly in car engines producing mainly carbon dioxide and water:

$$C_2H_5OH + 3O_2 \longrightarrow 2CO_2 + 3H_2O$$

Making and breaking esters

- Many alcohols and carboxylic acids used to prepare esters in the laboratory are highly flammable and no naked flame should be present during ester preparation.

Highly Flammable

- Methanol when warmed with methanoic acid (using concentrated H_2SO_4 as a catalyst) forms the ester called methyl methanoate.

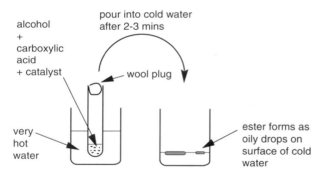

alcohol + carboxylic acid + catalyst

pour into cold water after 2-3 mins

wool plug

very hot water

ester forms as oily drops on surface of cold water

- The functional groups of the reactants (–OH and –COOH) take part in a condensation reaction to make water and allow the ester link to be made.

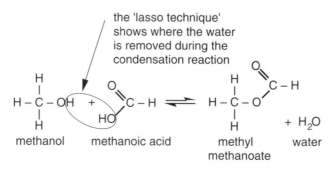

the 'lasso technique' shows where the water is removed during the condensation reaction

methanol   methanoic acid   methyl methanoate   water

$$CH_3OH + HOOCH \rightleftharpoons CH_3OOCH + H_2O$$

- Ester making is a reversible process.

- Ester hydrolysis converts an ester back into an alcohol and a carboxylic acid.

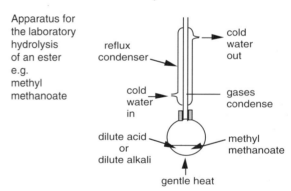

Apparatus for the laboratory hydrolysis of an ester e.g. methyl methanoate

reflux condenser

cold water out

cold water in

gases condense

dilute acid or dilute alkali

methyl methanoate

gentle heat

- The equation for ester hydrolysis also includes the reversible reaction sign.

$$CH_3OOCH + H_2O \rightleftharpoons CH_3OH + HCOOH$$

methyl methanoate   water   methanol   methanoic acid

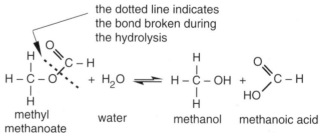

the dotted line indicates the bond broken during the hydrolysis

methyl methanoate   water   methanol   methanoic acid

- Many natural flavours and smells are due to volatile ester molecules in fruits and flowers.

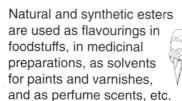

- Natural and synthetic esters are used as flavourings in foodstuffs, in medicinal preparations, as solvents for paints and varnishes, and as perfume scents, etc.

(d) Plastics and synthetic fibres

Uses

- Most plastics and fibres are synthetic or man-made materials produced by the chemical industries from chemicals isolated from crude oil and natural gas.

- Plastics have a great variety of everyday uses which are closely related to their chemical and their physical properties.

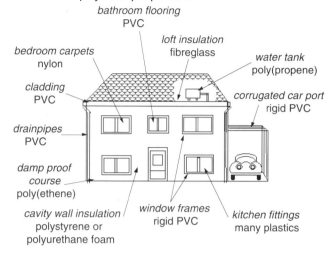

bathroom flooring
PVC

loft insulation
fibreglass

bedroom carpets
nylon

water tank
poly(propene)

cladding
PVC

corrugated car port
rigid PVC

drainpipes
PVC

damp proof
course
poly(ethene)

cavity wall insulation
polystyrene or
polyurethane foam

window frames
rigid PVC

kitchen fittings
many plastics

- Modern gloss and emulsion paints and home wallcoverings have plastic ingredients making surfaces hard-wearing and washable.

- Many sporting and leisure activities put plastics and fibres to good use!

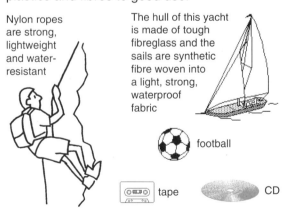

Nylon ropes are strong, lightweight and water-resistant

The hull of this yacht is made of tough fibreglass and the sails are synthetic fibre woven into a light, strong, waterproof fabric

football

tape   CD

- A list of plastics and fibres contains some very familiar terms and as chemists search for, and develop, new materials with special, improved properties, this list is forever expanding!

acrylic	bakelite	biopol	fibreglass
formica	kevlar	nylon	perspex
poly(ethene)	poly(propene)	polystyrene	PTFE
poly(ethenol)	polyester	polyurethane	PVC

[PVC, **p**oly**v**inyl **c**hloride, is known as poly(chloroethene)]

You should recognise some of these names but several may require further comment!

- Biopol is a biodegradable plastic developed in recent years by UK chemists.

- Kevlar, a really tough plastic made in recent years, has fibres stronger than steel wires.

- Poly(ethenol) is one of the few plastics which dissolves readily in water.

- Synthetic fibres include polyesters, nylons and acrylics.

- Natural fibres come from plants and animals, e.g. wool, silk, cotton and linen.

- Plastics and synthetic fibres can be specially designed by chemists to be 'substitutes' for natural materials such as wood, silk, cotton and wool.

- There are, of course, both advantages and disadvantages of natural v synthetic materials e.g. ease of drying.

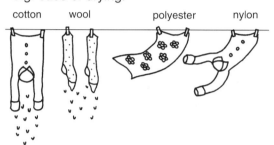

cotton   wool   polyester   nylon

- Some people just can not wear clothes made from synthetic fibres. They say that the natural 'feel' of cotton or wool or silk is far more comfortable than the synthetic goods.

- Most discarded plastics result in environmental pollution since they are low density and non-biodegradable i.e they do not decompose, like paper and wood, under the action of weather and bacteria.

- Regulations for fire-proofing of foam-filled, fibre-covered furnishings were introduced to reduce house deaths caused by inhalation of fumes from burning or smouldering items.

- The toxic gases released depend on the composition of the burning plastics. e.g.

most plastics → carbon monoxide
PVC → hydrogen chloride
polyurethane foam → hydrogen cyanide

- Plastics which can be melted and reshaped on heating are called thermoplastics.

AVOID HEAT

- Thermosetting plastics or thermosets do **not** resoften on heating.

- Thermosetting plastics are used for work surfaces, electric kettles, etc, where resistance to heat is essential e.g. Bakelite™ for plugs, power sockets and switches.

Addition polymerisation

- Many plastics are made from ethene, C_2H_4, and other alkenes obtained from the catalytic cracking of oil fractions.

- Poly(ethene) is probably the most widely used plastic ('Polythene' is a tradename).

- It is made by the addition polymerisation of ethene which involves joining up hundreds of small, unsaturated, C_2H_4 molecules to form a very large polymer chain.

ethene monomers → part of a poly(ethene) chain

- The polymer chain contains a repeating unit (see opposite) which has a C – C bond.
  This is formed as the C = C bond in the monomer molecule opens up to allow the unsaturated molecules to 'add' together using electrons from broken C = C bonds to form new bonds.

repeating unit for ethene

- The name of any addition polymer is clearly associated with the name of the monomer.
  i.e. ethene —> poly(ethene)
        propene —> poly(propene)

- Important addition polymers made from small, unsaturated, monomer molecules include:
  poly(chloroethene)   poly(propene)
  poly(phenylethene)   poly(tetrafluoroethene)

Remember, poly(chloroethene) is also known as PVC (polyvinylchloride) and poly(phenylethene) is also known as polystyrene.

chloroethene monomers → part of poly(chloroethene)

propene monomers → part of poly(propene)

tetrafluoroethene monomers → part of poly(tetrafluoroethene)

- An unsaturated monomer with the structural formula opposite, will always form an addition polymer chain with the structure:

part of polymer chain

and the saturated repeating unit:

Condensation polymerisation

- Many polymers, including polyamides (nylons) and polyesters are made from monomers with two functional groups per molecule.

- The functional groups on monomer molecules can react with functional groups on adjacent molecules to eliminate either water or some other small molecule and allow the monomers to join together in very long chains (polymers).

- The first polyamide condensation polymer was nylon-6,6 made from two different monomer molecules each having six carbon atoms.

- One monomer was a diamine (–NH_2 is the amine group); the other was a dicarboxylic acid (–COOH is the carboxyl group):

monomer 1   monomer 2   monomer 1

$+ NH_2(CH_2)_6NH_2 + HOOC(CH_2)_4COOH + NH_2(CH_2)_6NH_2 +$

↓

····· $-NH-(CH_2)_6-NH-C-(CH_2)_4-C-NH-(CH_2)_6-NH-$ ·····

part of the very large nylon–6,6 polymer chain

- The repeating group, –CONH–, is called the amide link and the polymers are polyamides.

- Amine and carboxyl groups may be present on a single monomer as in $NH_2(CH_2)_5COOH$.
  Can you see that condensation polymerisation of this monomer would give nylon-6?

- Polyesters may be formed by condensation polymerisation of a dicarboxylic acid (two –COOH groups present on each monomer molecule) and a diol (two –OH groups present on each monomer molecule).

- The different functional groups react together by eliminating water and forming ester links.

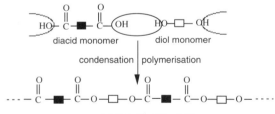

diacid monomer   diol monomer

condensation | polymerisation

part of a polyester chain

- Polyesters like Terylene™ produce long chains of linear polymers suitable for fibres.

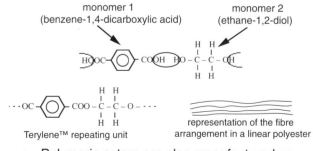

monomer 1
(benzene-1,4-dicarboxylic acid)

monomer 2
(ethane-1,2-diol)

Terylene™ repeating unit

representation of the fibre arrangement in a linear polyester

- Polymeric esters are also manufactured as polyester resins which, on setting (curing), have strong, rigid, three-dimensional structures.

representation of the cured resin structure

(e) Natural products

Carbohydrates

- We need energy to move, grow and keep warm.

- Carbohydrates (contain C,H and O only) are produced by plants during photosynthesis to provide us with important 'energy foods'.

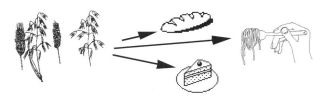

- Photosynthesis uses chlorophyll to absorb light energy from the sun and to convert the simple molecules of carbon dioxide and water into glucose (a sugar) and oxygen.

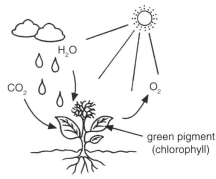

green pigment (chlorophyll)

- This complex process which stores the energy in the glucose is represented by:

$$6CO_2 + 6H_2O \longrightarrow C_6H_{12}O_6 + 6O_2$$
glucose

- Glucose, which is sweet and soluble in water, can undergo condensation polymerisation to form starches, which are not sweet and which do not dissolve well in water.

- Respiration is the process by which animals and plants obtain energy by breaking down carbohydrates:

$$C_6H_{12}O_6 + 6O_2 \longrightarrow 6CO_2 + 6H_2O$$
glucose

- The continuation of life on Earth depends on photosynthesis and respiration to maintain the balance of CO_2 and O_2 in the atmosphere.

- Burning fossil fuels worldwide has created a 'blanket' of CO_2 in the upper atmosphere which scientists believe is responsible for the small, observed increases in global temperatures over several years i.e. the 'greenhouse effect'.

- Climatic changes around the world may cause some islands and areas of coastline to totally 'disappear' as the oceans and seas expand!

- Clearing huge forested areas of all their green vegetation reduces both the uptake of CO_2 and the production of O_2 by photosynthesis!

- A general formula $C_x(H_2O)_y$ with H:O = 2:1, as in water, suggests 'hydrates of carbon', but carbohydrate structures are quite different!

- Sugars have smaller molecules than starches.

glucose ($C_6H_{12}O_6$)	maltose ($C_{12}H_{22}O_{11}$)
fructose ($C_6H_{12}O_6$)	sucrose ($C_{12}H_{22}O_{11}$)

Sucrose is ordinary cane or table sugar!

starches $(C_6H_{10}O_5)_n$ (n is ~25 to >1000 units)

- Carbohydrate molecules have really quite complicated structures and so you may find simplified representations useful e.g.

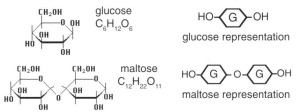

On examining ball models of some carbohydrate molecules, you will observe 'ring' structures.

- The number of 'rings' in sugars can be used to classify them as *monosaccharides* (one-ring):

HO–(G)–OH $C_6H_{12}O_6$ HO–(F)–OH

glucose and fructose are isomeric monosaccharides

or *disaccharides* (two-rings):

HO–(G)–O–(G)–OH   HO–(G)–O–(F)–OH

$C_{12}H_{22}O_{11}$

maltose and sucrose are isomeric disaccharides

- Starches can be classified as *polysaccharides* starting with around 25 glucose molecules linked by condensation, or with well over 1000 glucose molecules in the polymer chain.

- Green plants can make glucose monomer molecules lose water and form starches.

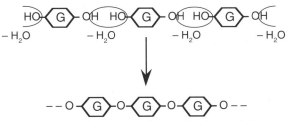

representation for part of a starch polymer chain

- Plants store energy by converting the glucose molecules into starches, and when energy is needed, enzymes break down the starches.

- Carbohydrates are also needed by plants for growing leaves, stems and other cellulose-like structures which provide them with support.

- Cellulose, a polymer larger than starch, has at least 3000 repeating –(G)–o units!

Reactions of carbohydrates

- Concentrated sulphuric acid, H_2SO_4, has such a powerful dehydrating action that it can remove the bonded H and O atoms from a carbohydrate, as H_2O, leaving only carbon!

TEACHER/LECTURER DEMONSTRATION

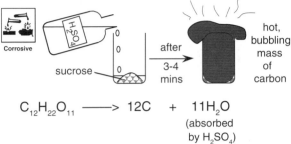

$$C_{12}H_{22}O_{11} \longrightarrow 12C + 11H_2O$$
(absorbed by H_2SO_4)

- The formation of CO_2 and H_2O from the burning of carbohydrates is evidence for the presence of the elements C and H.

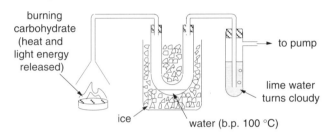

- Starch is distinguished from other common carbohydrates using iodine solution in a chemical test to produce a characteristic deep blue/black colour.

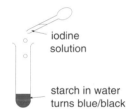

You may have encountered in earlier chemistry or biology studies that starch is not very soluble in water and does not really form a true solution!

- Starch in water is a colloid - not a true solution like glucose in water - and so it can produce the Tyndall effect, where light beams are dispersed by colloidal suspensions.

  The light beam from the torch produces a distinctive bright band of dispersed light called a Tyndall beam.

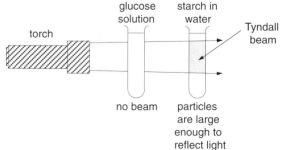

- Blue coloured Benedict's reagent turns an orange/red colour when warmed with most sugars e.g. glucose, fructose or maltose, but sucrose (also a sugar) is distinguished from the others by its negative result in this test.

Benedict's Test for Sugars

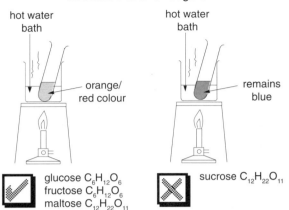

- Starch breaking down to glucose during digestion, by reacting with water in the presence of acid or enzymes, is called hydrolysis.

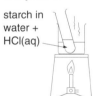

Glucose molecules are small enough to pass through the gut wall into the bloodstream and on to various parts of the body where cells use the glucose in respiration processes to provide energy.

- The hydrolysis of starch or large sugars can be carried out in the laboratory using acid or enzymes.

acid hydrolysis needs a high temperature

enzymes function well at body temperature and are destroyed at high temperatures

- Hydrolysis of sucrose produces two different sugars, glucose and fructose:

$$C_{12}H_{22}O_{11} + H_2O \longrightarrow C_6H_{12}O_6 + C_6H_{12}O_6$$
sucrose   water   glucose   fructose

- Paper chromatography is a useful technique for the identification of individual carbohydrates and for the separation and the identification of mixtures of carbohydrates.

Key to 'spotted' carbohydrates:
G – glucose; F – fructose;
Su – sucrose; H – products from sucrose hydrolysis

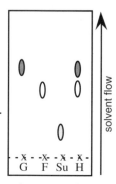

Proteins

- Protein formation takes place in nature by the absorption of nitrogen or nitrogen compounds.

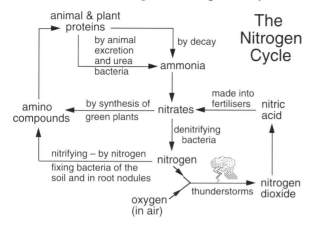

The Nitrogen Cycle

- We require proteins from animal and plant sources as essential foodstuffs in our diet for the growth and repair of body tissues.

- Animal tissues, body enzymes and a number of hormones are proteins, many with quite complex structures of intertwining and spiralling polypeptide chains.

But how did chemists first find out about the complex nature of protein structures?

- The discovery of the technique of paper chromatography led to the separation and identification of amino acids – the 'building blocks of proteins' – in the hydrolysis products (hydrolysates) of **all** proteins!

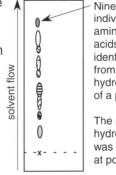

Nine individual amino acids identified from the hydrolysate of a protein.

The protein hydrolysate was 'spotted' at point x.

A developed chromatogram

- Representations may be used for an amino acid molecule.
  e.g.

amine group   carboxyl group

represents the other atoms in the molecule

- Of the twenty amino acids commonly found in proteins, most have both functional groups bonded to the same carbon atom.
  e.g.

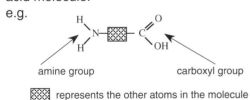

glycine   alanine   valine

- Different amino acid representations are often indicated by a change in the shaded block centre which has the amine and the carboxyl functional groups attached.
  e.g.

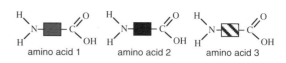

amino acid 1   amino acid 2   amino acid 3

- Proteins are condensation polymers of high molecular mass with several thousand amino acid monomer molecules bonded by peptide (amide) links in each protein molecule.

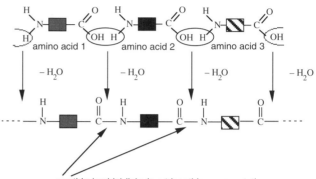

amino acid 1   amino acid 2   amino acid 3

$-H_2O$ $-H_2O$ $-H_2O$ $-H_2O$

peptide (amide) links in a tripeptide representation

- During digestion of our foods, body enzymes catalyse the hydrolysis of insoluble proteins to individual amino acid molecules.

- The smaller amino acids are then absorbed by the bloodstream and are circulated to the various parts of the body.

- Proteins specific to the body's needs are built up within our body cells from the amino acids released.

- Our body cells cannot make all the amino acids required for body proteins and so our body must obtain these so-called 'essential amino acids' from the proteins in our food.

- Hydrolysis of food proteins and condensation of the released amino acids by the body cells can be represented using a 'poppet bead' model.

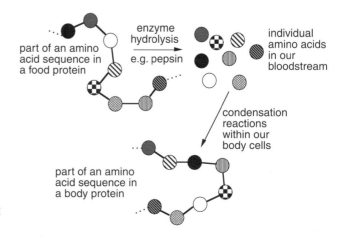

part of an amino acid sequence in a food protein

enzyme hydrolysis
e.g. pepsin

individual amino acids in our bloodstream

condensation reactions within our body cells

part of an amino acid sequence in a body protein

Fats and oils

- Supplies of fats and oils are found in many different plants and animals (including fish and other marine creatures).

- Animals generally produce fats which are mainly saturated solids or semi-solids; while plants and fish produce mainly unsaturated, liquid oils.

- Saturated molecules in fats tend to be more solid because they are able to bond more closely together than the unsaturated oil molecules.

- The lower melting points of oils compared to those of fats of similar molecular mass is related to the higher degree of unsaturation present in the oils.

- Fats and oils in the human diet provide a high energy source (more than double for the same mass of carbohydrate).

- Fats and oils are, however, also known to be essential for metabolic processes of the body.

- Some humans have diets with a high content of fats and oils with, apparently, few health problems!

- In recent years, medical research has suggested that there may be a link between heart disease (high in Scotland) and eating excessive amounts of saturated fatty foods.

- It has been suggested that the risk of heart disease is greatly reduced by eating fatty foods containing polyunsaturates i.e. fats with several C = C bonds in their molecules.

- Some recently published medical research, however, casts some doubt on the strength of this link.

- Generally, vegetable oils are a good source of polyunsaturates and fats are a poor source, although exceptions do exist e.g. coconut oil.

- Catalytic hydrogenation of vegetable oils forms compounds with the properties of animal fats and the conversion of liquid oils —> solid fats is the basis for the margarine industry.

- Unsaturated oils can have some C = C bonds saturated by the addition of hydrogen in the presence of a nickel catalyst.

$$---C=C--- + H_2 \xrightarrow[\text{catalyst}]{Ni} ---C-C---$$

unsaturated site in an 'oil molecule'   saturated site in a 'fat molecule'

- Naturally occurring fats and oils are, in fact, large esters.

- The ester molecules in oils and fats are made from glycerol and fatty acids in the ratio of glycerol : fatty acid = 1 : 3.

- Glycerol (propane-1,2,3-triol) is a trihydric alcohol i.e. each molecule has three hydroxyl (–OH) functional groups.

$$H - \underset{H}{\overset{OH}{C}} - \underset{H}{\overset{OH}{C}} - \underset{H}{\overset{OH}{C}} - H$$

glycerol

- Fatty acids can be saturated or unsaturated straight-chain carboxylic acids having even numbers of carbon atoms ranging from C_4 to C_{24}, but mainly C_{16} and C_{18}. e.g.

palmitic acid	$C_{15}H_{31}COOH$ (saturated)
oleic acid	$C_{17}H_{33}COOH$ (unsaturated)
stearic acid	$C_{17}H_{35}COOH$ (saturated)

- Esters formed from glycerol are also known as triglycerides e.g. glyceryl trioleate is typical of esters found in many oils.

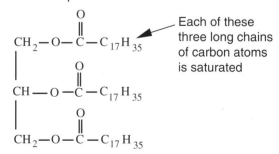

Each of these three long chains of carbon atoms has a C=C bond present i.e. an unsaturated group

- Hydrolysis of each glyceryl trioleate molecule produces one molecule of glycerol and three molecules of oleic acid, $C_{17}H_{33}COOH$.

- Glyceryl tristearate is typical of the saturated esters in plant and animal fats.

$$\begin{array}{l} CH_2-O-\overset{O}{\overset{\|}{C}}-C_{17}H_{35} \\ \quad\quad\quad\quad O \\ CH-O-\overset{\|}{C}-C_{17}H_{35} \\ \quad\quad\quad\quad O \\ CH_2-O-\overset{\|}{C}-C_{17}H_{35} \end{array}$$

Each of these three long chains of carbon atoms is saturated

- Hydrolysis of each glyceryl tristearate molecule produces one molecule of glycerol and three molecules of stearic acid, $C_{17}H_{35}COOH$.

(a) Acids and Bases

The pH scale

- The pH scale is a continuous range from below 0 to above 14 which identifies a solution as acidic, as alkaline or as neutral.

- The pH number of a solution can be found by using liquid or paper indicators or from a pH meter with a special electrode or probe.

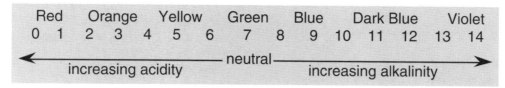

Red	Orange	Yellow	Green	Blue	Dark Blue	Violet
0 1	2 3	4 5	6 7	8 9	10 11 12	13 14

← increasing acidity — neutral — increasing alkalinity →

Sources of some acids and alkalis

- Some elements of the Periodic Table are classified as either metals or non-metals.

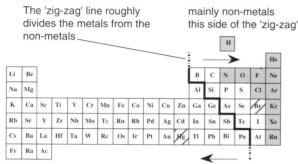

The 'zig-zag' line roughly divides the metals from the non-metals

mainly non-metals this side of the 'zig-zag'

mainly metals this side of the 'zig-zag'

- Some soluble non-metal oxides can form acids with water.
  e.g.

  sulphur dioxide + water —> sulphurous acid
  $$SO_2(g) + H_2O(l) \longrightarrow H_2SO_3(aq)$$

  carbon dioxide + water —> carbonic acid
  $$CO_2(g) + H_2O(l) \longrightarrow H_2CO_3(aq)$$

- Nitrogen dioxide, NO_2, made by sparking air is also an acidic oxide.

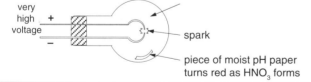

very high voltage

spark

piece of moist pH paper turns red as HNO_3 forms

- Soluble metal oxides (and soluble metal hydroxides) form alkalis when dissolved in water.
  e.g.

  sodium oxide + water —> sodium hydroxide
  $$Na_2O(s) + H_2O(l) \longrightarrow 2NaOH(aq)$$

- Some metals can react directly with water to form alkalis e.g. Group 1 elements.

  $$2K(s) + 2H_2O(l) \longrightarrow 2KOH(aq) + H_2(g)$$
  potassium   water   potassium hydroxide   hydrogen

- Ammonia gas, NH_3, can be made to dissolve in spectacular fashion to produce an alkali.

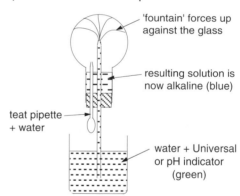

'fountain' forces up against the glass

resulting solution is now alkaline (blue)

teat pipette + water

water + Universal or pH indicator (green)

- Ammonia is very soluble in water forming the alkali called ammonium hydroxide.

$$NH_3(g) + H_2O(l) \rightleftharpoons NH_4^+(aq) + OH^-(aq)$$

Common acids and alkalis

- In the laboratory:

Acid	Formula
hydrochloric	$HCl(aq)$
sulphuric	$H_2SO_4(aq)$
nitric	$HNO_3(aq)$
ethanoic (acetic)	$CH_3COOH(aq)$

Alkali	Formula
sodium hydroxide	$NaOH(aq)$
potassium hydroxide	$KOH(aq)$
calcium hydroxide*	$Ca(OH)_2(aq)$
ammonia solution	$NH_3(aq)$

- In the home:

Acidic	Alkaline
vinegar **	toothpastes
fruits ***	indigestion remedies
fruit juices ***	household cleaners
milk ****	bleaches

*	also known as lime water
**	contains ethanoic (acetic) acid
***	contain citric acid
****	contains lactic acid

Water, aqueous solutions, ions and pH

- Pure water (pH = 7) conducts electricity only slightly since it contains low and equal concentrations of $H^+(aq)$ and $OH^-(aq)$ ions.

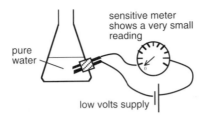

- Aqueous solutions also contain $H^+(aq)$ and $OH^-(aq)$ ions formed by the ionisation of a few water molecules.

$$H_2O(l) \rightleftharpoons H^+(aq) + OH^-(aq)$$

It is useful to use [ ] for 'the concentration of' ions in solution.

- When $[H^+] = [OH^-]$, the pH = 7, as in pure water and neutral aqueous solutions.

- Acidic solutions have more $H^+(aq)$ ions than pure water.
  i.e. $[H^+] > [OH^-]$ and the pH < 7.

- Alkaline solutions have more $OH^-(aq)$ ions than pure water.
  i.e. $[H^+] < [OH^-]$ and the pH > 7.

- Diluting an acidic solution reduces $[H^+]$ and the pH rises towards 7.

- Diluting an alkaline solution reduces $[OH^-]$ and the pH falls towards 7.

Chemical equilibrium

- When a chemical equation has a ' $\rightleftharpoons$ ' sign in place of the ' $\longrightarrow$ ' sign, it indicates the forward rate of reaction is exactly balanced by the reverse rate of reaction.

- In such situations, the two reactions are said to have reached, or to be in equilibrium.

- In pure water and in aqueous solutions, there is an equilibrium between water molecules and hydrogen and hydroxide ions:

$$H_2O(l) \rightleftharpoons H^+(aq) + OH^-(aq)$$

- Where equilibrium exists, the concentrations of 'reactants' and 'products' remain constant, although not necessarily equal!

- In water and in aqueous solutions, the H_2O molecules vastly outnumber H^+ and OH^- ions!

When you consider models for reaching an imaginary chemical equilibrium, for example:

$$P + Q \rightleftharpoons R + S$$

you should see that you would reach the same equilibrium whether you reacted P and Q (to make R and S) or if you reacted R and S (to make P and Q).

Concentration

- Chemists perform many experiments with chemicals dissolved in aqueous solution.

- The relative amounts of dissolved chemical (the solute) and water (the solvent) determine the concentration of the solution.

- Concentration units are expressed as moles per cubic decimetre, written as mol dm^{-3}.

$$1\ dm^3 = 1000\ cm^3$$

- A solution whose concentration is known is called a standard solution.

- A solution with a concentration of 1 mol dm^{-3} has 1 mole (1 mol) of chemical dissolved in water and made up to exactly 1 dm^3 of solution with more water.
  e.g. 1 mol dm^{-3} NaCl(aq) has 58.5 g NaCl dissolved in 1 dm^3 of solution.

- By taking different quantities of the chemicals and water it is possible to prepare any volume of solution of any concentration.

Study the following table and see if you can follow the relationships between moles of solute, volume of solution and concentration.

Moles (mol)	Volume (dm³)	Concentration (mol dm⁻³)
0.5	1.0	0.5
0.5	0.5	1.0
0.1	1.0	0.1
0.1	0.25	0.4
0.25	0.5	0.5

- $$\text{Concentration} = \frac{\text{moles}}{\text{volume}}$$

- $$\text{Moles} = \text{concentration} \times \text{volume}$$

- $$\text{Volume} = \frac{\text{moles}}{\text{concentration}}$$

You should also see the importance of being able to change the mass of a chemical into moles and volumes given in cm³ into dm³.

Strong and weak acids

- 'Strong' and 'weak' when applied to acids do not mean the same as concentrated and dilute!

- A strong acid is one which is fully ionised in solution e.g. $HCl(aq)$ - hydrochloric acid, $H_2SO_4(aq)$ - sulphuric acid, and $HNO_3(aq)$ - nitric acid.

- No acid molecules are present in solution as these are completely dissociated into ions. i.e.

$$HCl(aq) \longrightarrow H^+(aq) + Cl^-(aq)$$

$$HNO_3(aq) \longrightarrow H^+(aq) + NO_3^-(aq)$$

$$H_2SO_4(aq) \longrightarrow 2H^+(aq) + SO_4^{2-}(aq)$$

- A weak acid is one which is partially ionised in solution e.g. $CH_3COOH(aq)$ - ethanoic acid. i.e.

$$CH_3COOH(aq) \rightleftharpoons CH_3COO^-(aq) + H^+(aq)$$

- Equimolar solutions of strong and weak acids differ in pH, conductivity and reaction rates.

	$HCl(aq)$ (0.1 mol dm^{-3})	$CH_3COOH(aq)$ (0.1 mol dm^{-3})
pH	1	~3
Conductivity	high	low
Reaction rate (e.g. with Mg or $CaCO_3$ and the same set of variables)	fast	slow

Strong and weak bases

- 'Strong' and 'weak' when applied to bases do not mean the same as concentrated and dilute!

- A strong base is one which is fully ionised in solution e.g. aqueous solutions of the soluble metal hydroxides such as NaOH (sodium hydroxide) and KOH (potassium hydroxide). i.e.

$$NaOH(s) + aq \longrightarrow Na^+(aq) + OH^-(aq)$$

$$KOH(s) + aq \longrightarrow K^+(aq) + OH^-(aq)$$

- A weak base is one which is partially ionised in solution e.g. $NH_3(aq)$ - ammonia solution. i.e.

$$NH_3(g) + H_2O(l) \rightleftharpoons NH_4^+(aq) + OH^-(aq)$$

- Equimolar solutions of strong and weak bases differ in pH and conductivity.

	$NaOH(aq)$ (0.1 mol dm^{-3})	$NH_3(aq)$ (0.1 mol dm^{-3})
pH	14	~11
Conductivity	high	low

(b) Salt preparation

Reactions of acids (neutralisation)

- The reaction of acids with bases is called neutralisation.

- Metal oxides, metal carbonates and metal hydroxides are bases.

- Bases which are soluble in water produce solutions called alkalis.

- In the neutralisation of an acidic solution, the pH rises towards 7.

- In the neutralisation of an alkaline solution, the pH falls towards 7.

You will have carried out several types of neutralisations in your laboratory work.

acid + alkali —> salt + water

Hydrogen ions combine with hydroxide ions to form water:
$$H^+(aq) + OH^-(aq) \longrightarrow H_2O(l)$$

acid + metal oxide —> salt + water

Hydrogen ions and oxide ions combine to form water:
$$2H^+(aq) + O^{2-}(s) \longrightarrow H_2O(l)$$

acid + metal —> salt + water + carbon carbonate dioxide

Hydrogen ions and carbonate ions combine to form water and carbon dioxide:
$$2H^+(aq) + CO_3^{2-}(aq) \longrightarrow H_2O(l) + CO_2(g)$$

Neutralisation at work! *Your acid indigestion tablet experiments are safer and quicker neutralisations!*

Vinegar, a dilute solution of ethanoic acid, dabbed on the skin immediately following an alkaline wasp sting, can offer instant relief.

Helicopters regularly spray alkaline chemicals into lochs and lakes to counteract the effects of acid rain.

Gardeners add lime (CaO) to some plant soils to raise the pH to provide a more suitable growing medium for certain species.

Salts and hydrogen from acids

- Many acids can react with metals * to form salts and release hydrogen gas.

> **acid + metal * —> salt + hydrogen**
>
> Hydrogen ions in the acid are reduced to hydrogen gas molecules by electrons from the metal atoms:
> $$2H^+(aq) + 2e^- \longrightarrow H_2(g)$$

- * Only 'reactive' metals above hydrogen in the electrochemical series will behave in this way (see later).

- Hydrogen gas may be collected in an inverted test tube because it is much less dense than air.

- The identification test for hydrogen gas involves placing a lighted splint near the mouth of a test tube of the gas.

Explosive

- Hydrogen burns with a 'pop' i.e. a small explosion, to form water as the only product.

Acid rain

- Non-metal oxides like sulphur dioxide (SO_2) and nitrogen dioxide (NO_2) react with water in the atmosphere to produce acid rain.

- Coal- and oil-fired power stations (burning fossil fuels), oil refineries, metal ore smelters, factories and even house chimneys are the main sources of polluting sulphur dioxide.

- Cars with petrol engines spark air at very high temperatures producing nitrogen dioxide in their exhaust fumes.

- Acid rain attacks buildings and structures made from metals, concrete, limestone and marble causing expensive damage.

The Forth Rail Bridge

- Acid rain, or water made acid by this, causes a great deal of destruction to the natural environment. This can be seen in damage to soils, trees and the plant and animal life in lochs, lakes and rivers.

- Chemists are attempting to repair the acid rain damage by 'neutralising' the acid pollutants at source.

Volumetric titrations

- The technique of volumetric analysis may be used to exactly neutralise acidic or alkaline solutions.

- This involves titration using a pipette, burette, conical flask, indicator and the appropriate solutions.

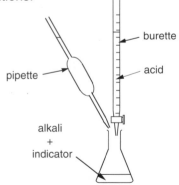

pipette — burette — acid — alkali + indicator

Do you remember all the procedures to follow?

(a) Rinse, and then fill the burette, with acid.
(b) Rinse, and then fill the pipette, with alkali.
(c) Discharge the volume of alkali from the pipette into the conical flask.
(d) Add a few drops of indicator to colour the contents of the conical flask.
(e) Run acid from the burette into the alkali and find the acid volume to exactly neutralise the known volume of alkali.

Most students agree that this is quite enjoyable experimental chemistry but the calculations to determine concentrations of either acid or alkali, from the results of volumetric titrations, are rarely described as an enjoyable experience!

Here's a useful equation to help in all cases!

Acid			Alkali		
V	× M × P	=	V	× M	× P

where V = volume; M = concentration; P = 'power'

The 'power' of an acid or alkali is the number of H^+ or OH^- ions involved in the neutralisation reaction.

e.g. HCl   P = 1; H_2SO_4 P = 2;
     NaOH P = 1; $Ca(OH)_2$ P = 2.

Check out this example calculation:

30 cm³ of 0.2 mol dm⁻³ sulphuric acid was exactly neutralised by 20 cm³ of a sodium hydroxide solution. Calculate the concentration of the alkali.

Acid			Alkali		
V	× M × P	=	V	× M	× P
30	× 0.2 × 2	=	20	× M	× 1

=> Concentration of alkali, M $= \dfrac{30 \times 0.2 \times 2}{20 \times 1}$

$= 0.6$ mol dm⁻³

Naming salts

- Salts are chemical compounds formed when the H^+ ions of acids are replaced by metal (or ammonium) ions.

- Hydrochloric acid, $HCl(aq)$, forms **chlorides**; sulphuric acid, $H_2SO_4(aq)$, forms **sulphates**; nitric acid, $HNO_3(aq)$; forms **nitrates** and the weak ethanoic acid, $CH_3COOH(aq)$, forms salts named **ethanoates**.

- The complete names of the salts formed in neutralisation reactions depend on individual reactants i.e. the acids can react with metals or bases.

Let's look at one example of each type of acid neutralisation reaction more closely and note the names of the salts formed in relation to the reactants used. Study the reaction equations too!

- Acid + metal

zinc + hydrochloric acid —> **zinc chloride** + hydrogen

$$Zn(s) \quad + \quad 2HCl(aq) \quad —> \quad ZnCl_2(aq) \quad + \quad H_2(g)$$

- Acid + metal oxide

nitric acid + copper(II) oxide —> **copper(II) nitrate** + water

$$2HNO_3(aq) + CuO(s) \quad —> \quad Cu(NO_3)_2(aq) + H_2O(l)$$

- Acid + metal carbonate

sulphuric + magnesium —> **magnesium** + water + carbon
acid   carbonate   **sulphate**   dioxide

$$H_2SO_4(aq) + MgCO_3(s) \quad —> \quad MgSO_4(aq) + H_2O(l) + CO_2(g)$$

- Acid + alkali

hydrochloric + potassium —> **potassium** + water
acid   hydroxide   **chloride**

$$HCl(aq) \quad + \quad KOH(aq) —> \quad KCl(aq) \quad + \quad H_2O(l)$$

Did you notice that all the salts formed in these reactions are soluble salts i.e. they are present in aqueous solution at the end of the neutralisation?

- In the formation of soluble salts, it is quite common to use an insoluble metal oxide or metal carbonate as the base.

- When an aqueous salt solution is the product of a neutralisation reaction, the solid salt may be recovered by evaporating most of the water and leaving the more concentrated salt solution formed to evaporate overnight. i.e.

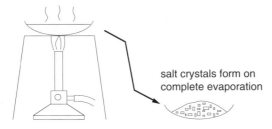

salt crystals form on complete evaporation

- A number of nitrogen-containing salts, such as nitrates and ammonium compounds, may be formed in neutralisation reactions with acids. e.g.

potassium nitrate formation:

$$HNO_3(aq) \quad + \quad KOH(aq) \quad —> \quad KNO_3(aq) \quad + \quad H_2O(l)$$

ammonium sulphate formation:

$$2NH_3(aq) \quad + \quad H_2SO_4(aq) \quad —> \quad (NH_4)_2SO_4(aq)$$

ammonium nitrate formation:

$$NH_3(aq) \quad + \quad HNO_3(aq) \quad —> \quad NH_4NO_3(aq)$$

- Such soluble nitrates and ammonium salts are in great demand as synthetic fertilisers along with potassium salts and phosphates of suitable solubility and nutrient composition.

- Fertilisers are substances which restore essential elements for plant growth to the soil.

- Plants require soluble nutrients including compounds of nitrogen, phosphorus and potassium. Different crops need different proportions of N, P and K.

- Although natural fertilisers form as a result of the breakdown of plant compost and animal manure, this is insufficient and the synthetic fertilisers made by expensive, large-scale neutralisations can replace the nutrients 'lost' as a result of modern farming methods.

- The rapid increase in world population means that greater efficiency is required in global food production and, consequently, fertiliser production and fertiliser usage will have to increase.

- However, caution must be observed in this area as over-application of fertilisers has already resulted in these being washed from the fields into drainage ditches, streams, rivers and lochs where they have created serious environmental pollution!

Dangerous to the Environment

Precipitation

- A check in Data Booklets on solubilities of compounds will reveal that many salts are insoluble in water.

- Insoluble salts can be formed by precipitation reactions where the insoluble product formed from the two solutions is called a precipitate. e.g.

barium + sulphuric —> barium + water
hydroxide   acid   sulphate

$Ba(OH)_2(aq) + H_2SO_4(aq) \longrightarrow BaSO_4(s) + 2H_2O(l)$

- Insoluble salts can be recovered by filtration and then dried, if required.

Ionic equations and spectator ions

- Neutralisation and precipitation reaction equations may be given in full ionic form.

e.g. $H^+(aq) + Cl^-(aq) + Na^+(aq) + OH^-(aq)$

$\longrightarrow H_2O(l) + Na^+(aq) + Cl^-(aq)$

- Sodium ions and chloride ions, which appear on both sides of the equation unchanged, are described as *spectator ions* and are often omitted from equations.

i.e. $H^+(aq) + Cl^-\cancel{(aq)} + Na^+\cancel{(aq)} + OH^-(aq)$

$\longrightarrow H_2O(l) + Na^+\cancel{(aq)} + Cl^-\cancel{(aq)}$

- The equation, minus spectator ions, is written:

$$H^+(aq) + OH^-(aq) \longrightarrow H_2O(l)$$

(c) Metals

Electricity from chemicals

- Any device which creates electricity from a chemical reaction is called a cell, symbol ⊣⊢

- Electricity passing through metals is a flow of electrons.

- The simplest cells producing a small voltage use two different metals and an electrolyte. e.g.

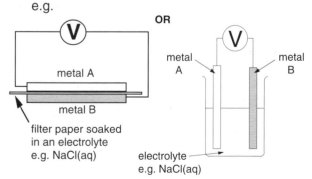

- The purpose of the electrolyte is to complete the circuit by allowing ions to carry charges between the two metal strips or electrodes.

Did you experiment with a 'lemon cell'?
The acidic juices make an ideal electrolyte!

- Lead(II) iodide may be prepared by reacting lead(II) nitrate solution with potassium iodide solution:

$Pb(NO_3)_2(aq) + 2KI(aq) \longrightarrow PbI_2(s) + 2KNO_3(aq)$

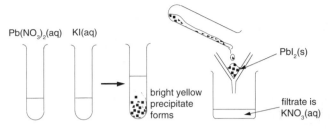

Which soluble salt is present in the filtrate?

- The full ionic equation for the preparation of lead(II) iodide is given as:

$Pb^{2+}(aq) + 2NO_3^-(aq) + 2K^+(aq) + 2I^-(aq)$

$\longrightarrow Pb^{2+}(I^-)_2(s) + 2K^+(aq) + 2NO_3^-(aq)$

- In this reaction, it is the potassium ions and the nitrate ions which are the spectator ions, appearing on both sides of the equation unchanged.

- When these spectator ions are omitted:

$Pb^{2+}(aq) + 2\cancel{NO_3^-}(aq) + 2\cancel{K^+}(aq) + 2I^-(aq)$

$\longrightarrow Pb^{2+}(I^-)_2(s) + 2\cancel{K^+}(aq) + 2\cancel{NO_3^-}(aq)$

the equation may be written as:

$$Pb^{2+}(aq) + 2I^-(aq) \longrightarrow Pb^{2+}(I^-)_2(s)$$

- Cells and batteries produce electricity from chemical reactions.

- A battery is made from several cells joined together.

- We rely greatly on mains electricity and batteries in our everyday lives!

- Scarce resources of fossil fuels are used up to produce mains electricity in power stations.

- Most batteries need to be replaced when the chemicals – mainly metals – taking part in the chemical reactions are used up.

Chemical energy —> electrical energy

- Some batteries are rechargeable. e.g. car batteries.

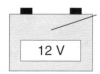

lead and lead oxide coated plates act as electrodes with sulphuric acid as the electrolyte

Electrical energy —> chemical energy (during the recharging stage)

An Electrochemical Series

You will have seen in simple cells that pairs of different metals produce different voltages.

- An electrochemical series of metals can be established by setting up several metal-pair cells and noting the voltage and the direction of electron flow.

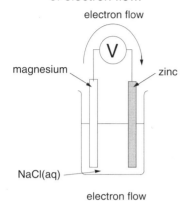

The Mg/Zn cell

V = 1.5 v

Electrons flow from the magnesium to the zinc through the voltmeter (the external circuit).

Mg is higher up in the electrochemical series than Zn.

The Zn/Cu cell

V = 1.1 v

Electrons flow from the zinc to the copper through the voltmeter (the external circuit).

Zn is higher up in the electrochemical series than Cu.

- From the cell voltages and the directions of the electron flow, the placing of these three metals in the electrochemical series is .... Mg > Zn > Cu ....

- By making cells of many different pairs of metals, it is possible to obtain a fuller electrochemical series.

- A pattern is found among the cell voltage measurements taken in these experiments.

- The closer the pair of metals are to each other in the electrochemical series, the smaller is the cell voltage obtained.

- The further apart the pair of metals are in the electrochemical series, the greater is the cell voltage obtained.

Can you see that, using the values opposite, the voltage for a Mg/Cu metal-pair cell would be 2.6 v?

- A shortened electrochemical series containing only a few well-known metals is given below:

Ca > Mg > Al > Zn > Fe > Sn > Pb > Cu > Hg > Ag > Au

- The electrochemical series resembles the reactivity series of metals (see later).

Displacement reactions and redox

- When metals are placed in solutions of other metal ions, reactions may take place to form, or displace, the other metal from its ions.

- A clear pattern is established from the results of displacement experiments.

- A metal higher up in the electrochemical series than another metal, can displace the metal lower down in the series from a solution of its ions.
  e.g. zinc can displace copper from a solution containing copper(II) ions.

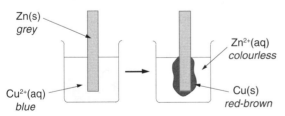

- It is not possible for any metal in the electrochemical series to displace a 'higher placed' metal from a solution of its ions. i.e. copper cannot displace zinc from a solution containing zinc ions.

NO REACTION

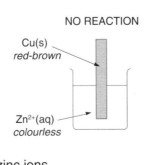

- The terms **oxidation** (a loss of electrons by any reactant), **reduction** (a gain of electrons by any reactant) and **redox** (reduction and oxidation taking place together) are used by chemists in descriptions of chemical reactions where electrons have been transferred.

- When zinc displaces copper from a solution containing copper(II) ions, the zinc (the higher placed metal) goes into solution as zinc ions as its atoms lose electrons:

$$Zn(s) \longrightarrow Zn^{2+}(aq) + 2e^- \quad \text{Oxidation}$$

- Ions of the lower placed metal i.e. copper, gain these electrons and form copper atoms:

$$Cu^{2+}(aq) + 2e^- \longrightarrow Cu(s) \quad \text{Reduction}$$

- The overall result is electron transfer from the higher placed metal, zinc, to the $Cu^{2+}(aq)$ ions i.e. the ions of the lower placed metal.

- The overall chemical reaction equation is obtained by adding the two steps:

$$Zn(s) \longrightarrow Zn^{2+}(aq) + \cancel{2e^-}$$
$$Cu^{2+}(aq) + \cancel{2e^-} \longrightarrow Cu(s)$$
$$\overline{Zn(s) + Cu^{2+}(aq) \longrightarrow Zn^{2+}(aq) + Cu(s)}$$

- This is the equation representing the *redox reaction* – reduction and oxidation taking place together – which has taken place to bring about the displacement of copper.

Hydrogen in the electrochemical series

- Reacting metals with acids can establish the position of hydrogen in the electrochemical series.

- When hydrogen is displaced from a metal/acid reaction, the metal is higher placed in the series than hydrogen.
  e.g.

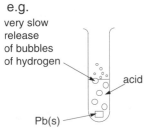

very slow release of bubbles of hydrogen

acid

Pb(s)

Lead is oxidised to lead ions:

$$Pb(s) \longrightarrow Pb^{2+}(aq) + 2e^-$$

Hydrogen ions are reduced to hydrogen:

$$2H^+(aq) + 2e^- \longrightarrow H_2(g)$$

- When a metal cannot displace hydrogen gas from an acid, the metal must be lower in the electrochemical series than hydrogen.
  e.g.

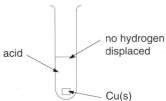

acid

no hydrogen displaced

Cu(s)

- The results of these two experiments would confirm the electrochemical series order for these three elements as:

$$.... Pb > H > Cu ....$$

Metal/metal ion cells

- Metals do not react with their own ions!

- Chemists can study the electron flow in redox reactions in cells made from two half-cells.
  e.g.

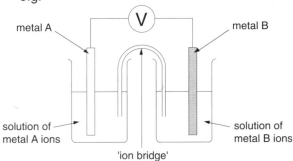

metal A

metal B

solution of metal A ions

solution of metal B ions

'ion bridge'

- The 'ion bridge' (sometimes known as a 'salt bridge') completes the circuit by allowing ions to flow between the two solutions.

- These cells may be set up to study redox reactions by combining any two metal/metal ion half-cells in this way.

- The size of the cell voltage depends on the two metal/metal ion half-cells put together.

Consider how electricity is produced in this cell.

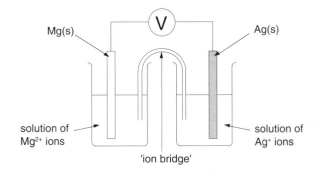

Mg(s)

Ag(s)

solution of Mg^{2+} ions

solution of Ag^+ ions

'ion bridge'

- The electron flow in the external circuit is from $Mg \longrightarrow Ag$.

- Mg is higher up in the electrochemical series than Ag.

- The oxidation taking place is:
  $$Mg(s) \longrightarrow Mg^{2+}(aq) + 2e^-$$

- The reduction taking place is:
  $$2Ag^+(aq) + 2e^- \longrightarrow 2Ag(s)$$

- The redox reaction equation is:
  $$Mg(s) + 2Ag^+(aq) \longrightarrow Mg^{2+}(aq) + 2Ag(s)$$

Half-cells without metals

- Cells involving redox reactions need not have two metal/metal ion half-cells.

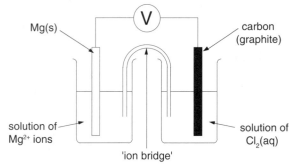

Mg(s)

carbon (graphite)

solution of Mg^{2+} ions

solution of Cl_2(aq)

'ion bridge'

The cell oxidation and reduction reactions are:

$$Mg(s) \longrightarrow Mg^{2+}(aq) + 2e^- \qquad \text{(Ox)}$$
and,
$$Cl_2(aq) + 2e^- \longrightarrow 2Cl^-(aq) \qquad \text{(Red)}$$

- In fact, cells involving redox reactions need not have any metal/metal ion half-cells!

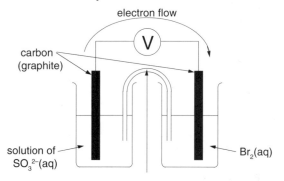

electron flow

carbon (graphite)

solution of SO_3^{2-}(aq)

Br_2(aq)

The cell oxidation and reduction reactions are:

$$SO_3^{2-}(aq) + H_2O(l) \longrightarrow SO_4^{2-}(aq) + 2H^+(aq) + 2e^- \text{ (Ox)}$$
and,
$$Br_2(aq) + 2e^- \longrightarrow 2Br^-(aq) \qquad \text{(Red)}$$

More balanced redox equations

It was the combination of the oxidation step ion-electron equation with the reduction step ion-electron equation, after balancing for the number of electrons 'lost' and 'gained' by the reaction species, which resulted in:

$$Mg(s) + 2Ag^+(aq) \longrightarrow Mg^{2+}(aq) + 2Ag(s)$$ *i.e. the balanced redox equation for the Mg/Ag cell.*
(See previous page).

Can you see how the following balanced redox equations are formed from the oxidation and reduction step ion-electron equations in each of these reactions?

Reaction 1

$$Mg(s) \longrightarrow Mg^{2+}(aq) + 2e^-$$

$$Cl_2(aq) + 2e^- \longrightarrow 2Cl^-(aq)$$

$$Mg(s) + Cl_2(aq) \longrightarrow Mg^{2+}(aq) + 2Cl^-(aq)$$

Reaction 2

$$SO_3^{2-}(aq) + H_2O(l) \longrightarrow SO_4^{2-}(aq) + 2H^+(aq) + 2e^-$$

$$Br_2(aq) + 2e^- \longrightarrow 2Br^-(aq)$$

$$SO_3^{2-}(aq) + H_2O(l) + Br_2(aq) \longrightarrow SO_4^{2-}(aq) + 2H^+(aq) + 2Br^-(aq)$$

Just in case you think that $2e^-$ are always involved in the oxidation and reduction steps, take a look at how the balancing of electrons is achieved in the next two reactions!

Reaction 3

$Cr_2O_7^{2-}/Fe^{2+}$ reaction   (**state symbols omitted**)

$$Fe^{2+} \longrightarrow Fe^{3+} + e^- \qquad \text{(oxidation)}$$

$$Cr_2O_7^{2-} + 14H^+ + 6e^- \longrightarrow 2Cr^{3+} + 7H_2O \quad \text{(reduction)}$$

Balance the number of electrons in the oxidation and reduction ion-electron equations and add!

$$6Fe^{2+} \longrightarrow 6Fe^{3+} + 6e^-$$

$$Cr_2O_7^{2-} + 14H^+ + 6e^- \longrightarrow 2Cr^{3+} + 7H_2O$$

$$Cr_2O_7^{2-} + 14H^+ + 6Fe^{2+} \longrightarrow 2Cr^{3+} + 6Fe^{3+} + 7H_2O$$

Reaction 4

MnO_4^-/Fe^{2+} reaction   (**state symbols omitted**)

$$Fe^{2+} \longrightarrow Fe^{3+} + e^- \qquad \text{(oxidation)}$$

$$MnO_4^- + 8H^+ + 5e^- \longrightarrow Mn^{2+} + 4H_2O \quad \text{(reduction)}$$

Balance the number of electrons in the oxidation and reduction ion-electron equations and add!

$$5Fe^{2+} \longrightarrow 5Fe^{3+} + 5e^-$$

$$MnO_4^- + 8H^+ + 5e^- \longrightarrow Mn^{2+} + 4H_2O$$

$$MnO_4^- + 8H^+ + 5Fe^{2+} \longrightarrow Mn^{2+} + 5Fe^{3+} + 4H_2O$$

Electrolysis cells

In the redox cells encountered earlier, electricity was made by the chemical reactants undergoing the chemical changes of oxidation and reduction to bring about a flow of electrons.

*However, in electrolysis, the **reverse** applies! Electricity is supplied to a melt (a molten substance) or an aqueous solution, through electrodes, to bring about the chemical changes of oxidation and reduction at the electrodes where ions are discharged and undergo chemical changes.*

Electrolysis of hydrochloric acid	**Electrolysis of molten lead iodide**	**Electrolysis of copper chloride (aq)**
Ions discharged: $H^+(aq)$ and $Cl^-(aq)$	Ions discharged: $Pb^{2+}(l)$ and $I^-(l)$	Ions discharged: $Cu^{2+}(aq)$ and $Cl^-(aq)$
During electrolysis, $H^+(aq)$ ions migrate towards the negative electrode (cathode) and $Cl^-(aq)$ ions migrate towards the positive electrode (anode).	During electrolysis, $Pb^{2+}(l)$ ions migrate towards the negative electrode (cathode) and $I^-(l)$ ions migrate towards the positive electrode (anode).	During electrolysis, $Cu^{2+}(aq)$ ions migrate towards the negative electrode (cathode) and $Cl^-(aq)$ ions migrate towards the positive electrode (anode).
At the cathode (–):	At the cathode (–):	At the cathode (–):
$2H^+(aq) + 2e^- \longrightarrow H_2(g)$	$Pb^{2+}(l) + 2e^- \longrightarrow Pb(l)$	$Cu^{2+}(aq) + 2e^- \longrightarrow Cu(s)$
This is the **reduction** of hydrogen ions to hydrogen molecules.	This is the **reduction** of lead(II) ions to lead atoms.	This is the **reduction** of copper(II) ions to copper atoms.
At the anode (+):	At the anode (+):	At the anode (+):
$2Cl^-(aq) \longrightarrow Cl_2(g) + 2e^-$	$2I^-(l) \longrightarrow I_2(g) + 2e^-$	$2Cl^-(aq) \longrightarrow Cl_2(g) + 2e^-$
This is the **oxidation** of chloride ions to chlorine molecules.	This is the **oxidation** of iodide ions to iodine molecules.	This is the **oxidation** of chloride ions to chlorine molecules.

Reactions of metals

- A reactivity series of metals can be established by observing in the laboratory, the reactions of a range of metals with oxygen, water and dilute acid.

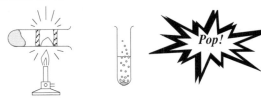

The amount of energy needed, or released, in metal reactions with oxygen, water and dilute acid should help you to clarify the relationship between the reactivity of metals and the stability of their compounds made in reactions.

When very reactive metals take part in reactions, usually a lot of energy is released to form very stable metal compounds which are very difficult to break up again. Fairly unreactive metals form less stable compounds with more difficulty but these compounds are broken down more easily.

Metals and oxygen

- The Group I metals are stored under light oil because they react instantly with oxygen in the air to form metal oxides.

- Word equations or chemical equations indicate what has happened during such combustions.
  e.g.
  potassium + oxygen ⟶ potassium oxide

  $$4K(s) \ + \ O_2(g) \longrightarrow 2K_2O(s)$$

Your chemistry teacher or lecturer may have shown you a number of metal powders reacting with oxygen in the laboratory using the following apparatus:

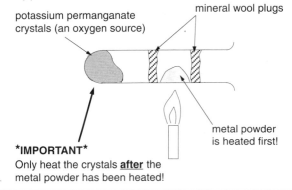

potassium permanganate crystals (an oxygen source)

mineral wool plugs

metal powder is heated first!

IMPORTANT
Only heat the crystals **after** the metal powder has been heated!

- Magnesium burns very vigorously in oxygen with a brilliant white light! Mg is very reactive!

  magnesium + oxygen ⟶ magnesium oxide

  $$2Mg(s) \ + \ O_2(g) \longrightarrow 2MgO(s)$$

- Zinc reacts very quickly releasing a lot of heat and light energy! Zn is quite reactive!

  zinc + oxygen ⟶ zinc oxide

  $$2Zn(s) \ + \ O_2(g) \longrightarrow 2ZnO(s)$$

- Iron reacts quite quickly releasing less heat and light energy. Fe is moderately reactive!

  iron + oxygen ⟶ iron(III) oxide

  $$4Fe(s) \ + \ 3O_2(g) \longrightarrow 2Fe_2O_3(s)$$

- Copper reacts but only 'glows' during the reaction. Cu is a less reactive metal.

  copper + oxygen ⟶ copper(II) oxide

  $$2Cu(s) \ + \ O_2(g) \longrightarrow 2CuO(s)$$

- So far, you would have a metal reactivity order:

  .... Mg > Zn > Fe > Cu ....

Metals and water

- The Group I metals react violently with cold water and must be stored safely under light oil.
  e.g.
  Explosive
  potassium + water ⟶ potassium + hydrogen hydroxide

  $$2K(s) \ + \ 2H_2O(l) \longrightarrow 2KOH(aq) \ + \ H_2(g)$$

- Calcium reacts quite strongly in cold water.

  $$Ca(s) + 2H_2O(l) \longrightarrow Ca(OH)_2(aq) + H_2(g)$$

  calcium + water ⟶ calcium + hydrogen hydroxide

- From comparisons of metal reactivities with cold water, the reactivity series now has:

  .... K > Na > Li > Ca > Mg ....

Metals and acid   *Note: K, Na, Li and Ca are **never added to acids** – the reactions are far too violent!*

- From metals placed in acid, a reactivity order can be determined by the rate of the release of hydrogen gas ('the bubbling rate').

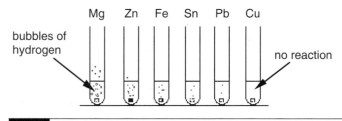

bubbles of hydrogen

no reaction

- Magnesium reacts quickly in acid!

  $$Mg(s) + 2HCl(aq) \longrightarrow H_2(g) + MgCl_2(aq)$$

- Zinc reacts more slowly in acid!

  $$Zn(s) + 2HCl(aq) \longrightarrow H_2(g) + ZnCl_2(aq)$$

- Lead reacts very slowly in warm acid!

  $$Pb(s) + 2HCl(aq) \longrightarrow H_2(g) + PbCl_2(s)$$

- Copper does not displace hydrogen from acid.

A reactivity series

- By combining all the results from other experiments on a wider range of metals with oxygen, water and dilute acid, a reactivity series of metals is formed.

$$K > Na > Li > Ca > Mg > Al > Zn > Fe > Sn > Pb > \boxed{H} > Cu > Hg > Ag > Au > Pt$$

potassium sodium lithium calcium magnesium aluminium zinc iron tin lead hydrogen copper mercury silver gold platinum

MOST
REACTIVE ⟶ LEAST
REACTIVE

MOST
STABLE
COMPOUNDS ⟶ LEAST
STABLE
COMPOUNDS

Metal ores

- There was a great deal of energy around when chemicals were first forming the Earth's crust many millions of years ago!

- Chemical substances did not all react with the same vigour!

- The less reactive metals did not combine readily with other elements such as oxygen, carbon and sulphur to form compounds.

- Unreactive metals are still found uncombined (native) in the Earth's crust e.g. Cu,Ag, Au, Pt.

- For this reason, many early civilisations 'discovered', and made great use of, these less reactive native metals.

- Most metals are found in nature as ores – naturally occurring, impure mixtures of the metal compounds.

- The more reactive metals are not found as uncombined elements and have to be extracted from their various ores.

- Some metal ores contain a very high proportion of waste matter e.g. to produce a single tonne of copper could require treatment of one hundred tonnes of a copper ore!

- The discovery of chemical extraction methods to reduce metal compounds to metals was necessary before man could isolate and make use of the wide range of metals.

- Unstable compounds of some less reactive metals may be reduced to metal on heating the ore.

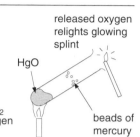

released oxygen relights glowing splint

HgO

beads of mercury

$$2HgO \longrightarrow 2Hg + O_2$$
mercury(II)   mercury   oxygen
oxide

- The industrial revolution of the 19th century demanded more machinery and so a higher production of iron and steel followed.

- Iron is produced from iron ore (Fe_2O_3) in blast furnaces.

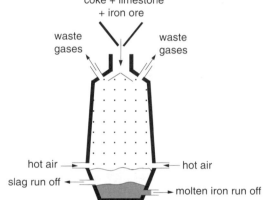

coke + limestone + iron ore

waste gases

waste gases

hot air — — hot air

slag run off ◄—

molten iron run off

Key reactions: (1) making CO; (2) reducing Fe_2O_3

$$\left. \begin{array}{l} C + O_2 \longrightarrow CO_2 \\ CO_2 + C \longrightarrow 2CO \end{array} \right\} \cdots (1)$$

$$Fe_2O_3 + 3CO \longrightarrow 2Fe + 3CO_2 \cdots (2)$$

The CO is the reducing agent in the reaction.

- Modern industries and a healthy consumer society still ensure a very high demand for the more reactive metals e.g. aluminium.

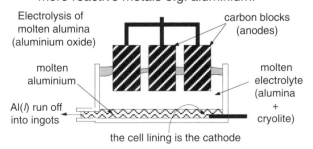

Electrolysis of molten alumina (aluminium oxide)

carbon blocks (anodes)

molten aluminium

molten electrolyte (alumina + cryolite)

Al(l) run off into ingots

the cell lining is the cathode

- The reduction taking place at the cathode is:

$$Al^{3+}(l) + 3e^- \longrightarrow Al(l)$$

Corrosion

- Corrosion is a chemical reaction which involves changes on the surface of a metal converting it from an element to a compound.

- Generally, the more reactive the metal, the faster the speed of corrosion.

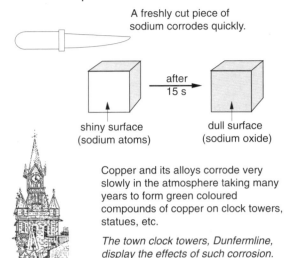

A freshly cut piece of sodium corrodes quickly.

after 15 s

shiny surface (sodium atoms) → dull surface (sodium oxide)

Copper and its alloys corrode very slowly in the atmosphere taking many years to form green coloured compounds of copper on clock towers, statues, etc.

The town clock towers, Dunfermline, display the effects of such corrosion.

- The corrosion process of metals involves the oxidation of metal atoms.
  e.g. the corrosion of iron

$$Fe \longrightarrow Fe^{2+} + 2e^-$$

The chemistry of rusting

- When iron rusts, iron atoms initially 'lose electrons' forming iron(II) ions:

$$Fe \longrightarrow Fe^{2+} + 2e^- \qquad \text{Oxidation}$$

- Iron(II) ions can be further oxidised by losing electrons to form iron(III) ions:

$$Fe^{2+} \longrightarrow Fe^{3+} + e^- \qquad \text{Oxidation}$$

- The electrons 'lost' during these oxidation reactions are, of course, gained by the water and oxygen (in the air) to form hydroxide ions:

$$2H_2O + O_2 + 4e^- \longrightarrow 4OH^- \qquad \text{Reduction}$$

- The Fe^{2+} and Fe^{3+} ions formed during the rusting of iron (and steel) can be identified by simple chemical tests.

Fe^{2+}	**Ferroxyl indicator turns dark blue.**

Fe^{3+}	**Thiocyanate indicator turns blood red.**

OH^-	**Ferroxyl indicator turns pink.**

- The corrosion of iron (and steel) is called rusting.

You probably set up test tube experiments with iron nails under different conditions and left them for several days before examining them for any evidence of rusting.

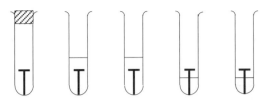

nails in air only, boiled water, water and air, salt water, acid, etc.

- Water, H_2O, and oxygen, O_2, (from the air) in the presence of an electrolyte (water contains dissolved CO_2) are all required for the rusting of iron to take place.

- Salt (an electrolyte) is used mixed with grit and sand to be spread on icy roads in the winter months.

- This increases the rusting of the undersides of cars and also car bodywork panels and, if not washed away, will eventually prove to be costly to the motorist!

- Ferroxyl indicator contains both ferricyanide and phenolphthalein.

- Experiments set up to investigate the rusting of iron nails provide evidence for electron flow from iron to carbon impurities during the rusting process and also for the formation of iron(II) ions and hydroxide ions.
  e.g.

electron flow

A meter

large iron nail

carbon (graphite) electrode

salt water + ferroxyl indicator

- A dark blue colouration forms around the nail where it is immersed. Fe^{2+} ions have been detected by the indicator.

$$Fe \longrightarrow Fe^{2+} + 2e^-$$

- A pink colouration forms around the carbon electrode where it is immersed. OH^- ions have been detected by the indicator.

$$2H_2O + O_2 + 4e^- \longrightarrow 4OH^-$$

Preventing corrosion

- Oxidation is the natural tendency for the more reactive metals and so corrosion of some metals can never be stopped – it can only be slowed down!

- Acid rain accelerates the corrosion of metals.

- Surface barriers to air, water and electrolytes can provide a degree of **physical protection** against corrosion.

- For example:

  painting

  oiling or greasing

  coating with plastic

  coating with another metal.

Protective metal layers

- Experiments involving different metal strips attached to iron nails show that some metals provide iron with **electrochemical protection**.

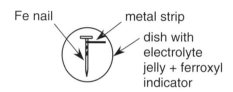

Fe nail   metal strip

dish with electrolyte jelly + ferroxyl indicator

Experimental observations:

- With Mg strip, no corrosion of Fe nail but Mg strip corroded badly.

- With Zn strip, no corrosion of Fe nail but Zn strip corroded badly.

- With Sn strip, Fe nail corroded badly but Sn strip not corroded.

- With Cu strip, Fe nail corroded badly but Cu strip not corroded.

Conclusions:

- Metals higher in the electrochemical series than Fe form ions more readily than Fe.

- Iron in metal-pair cells with metals higher in the electrochemical series than Fe, has electrons flowing on to the iron preventing the oxidation (rusting) of Fe atoms.

- Iron in metal-pair cells with metals lower in the electrochemical series than Fe, has electrons flowing from the iron increasing the corrosion (rusting) rate of Fe atoms.

- Iron becomes **galvanised** (Zn coated) by dipping in molten zinc.

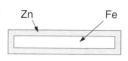

- The Zn coating offers both physical and electrochemical protection and it continues to supply an electron flow on to the iron even when the zinc surface is scratched.

- **Tin-plating** is resistant to attack by air and water and can physically protect an iron or a steel surface. However, if the tin surface is broken or scratched, the iron corrodes very quickly as electrons flow from Fe to Sn thus increasing the $Fe \longrightarrow Fe^{2+} + 2e^-$ reaction (oxidation).

- Copper, nickel or chromium may be **electroplated** on to iron or steel by making the iron object the cathode during an electrolysis reaction. e.g. nickel plating.

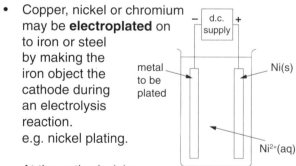

At the cathode (–):

$$Ni^{2+}(aq) + 2e^- \longrightarrow Ni(s) \qquad \text{Reduction}$$

A nickel anode (+) maintains the $[Ni^{2+}(aq)]$:

$$Ni(s) \longrightarrow Ni^{2+}(aq) + 2e^- \qquad \text{Oxidation}$$

Anti-corrosion methods in action
Sacrificial protection

- This takes place when one metal is allowed to corrode i.e. it is 'sacrificed' to supply its electrons to iron so that the iron does not rust. e.g.

Zn plates on side of ship's hull

$Zn \longrightarrow Zn^{2+} + 2e^-$

Fe pipe

bag of scrap Mg metal linked to underground pipe

$Mg \longrightarrow Mg^{2+} + 2e^-$

Cathodic protection

- A flow of electrons is supplied to an iron or steel object from a negative (cathode) supply.

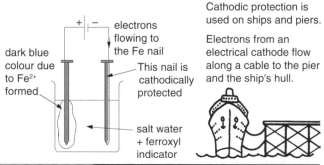

dark blue colour due to Fe^{2+} formed

electrons flowing to the Fe nail

This nail is cathodically protected

salt water + ferroxyl indicator

Cathodic protection is used on ships and piers.

Electrons from an electrical cathode flow along a cable to the pier and the ship's hull.

Unit 1   Building Blocks — Intermediate 2

Contents	Page	Commenced	Completed	Revision 1	Revision 2
(a) Substances	4				
Elements		/ /	/ /	/ /	/ /
The Periodic Table		/ /	/ /	/ /	/ /
Uses of elements	5	/ /	/ /	/ /	/ /
Reactions of the Group 1 elements		/ /	/ /	/ /	/ /
Making and naming compounds		/ /	/ /	/ /	/ /
Chemical Reactions	6	/ /	/ /	/ /	/ /
Mixtures		/ /	/ /	/ /	/ /
Solutions	7	/ /	/ /	/ /	/ /
(b) Reaction rates					
Following the course of a reaction		/ /	/ /	/ /	/ /
Calculating the average rate of reaction	8	/ /	/ /	/ /	/ /
Collision theory		/ /	/ /	/ /	/ /
Factors affecting rate of reaction		/ /	/ /	/ /	/ /
Change in concentration		/ /	/ /	/ /	/ /
Change in particle size	9	/ /	/ /	/ /	/ /
Change in temperature		/ /	/ /	/ /	/ /
Some everyday chemical reactions and rate variables		/ /	/ /	/ /	/ /
Catalysts	10	/ /	/ /	/ /	/ /
Catalyst surfaces at work		/ /	/ /	/ /	/ /
Enzymes - biological catalysts		/ /	/ /	/ /	/ /
(c) The structure of the atom	11				
Sub-atomic particles		/ /	/ /	/ /	/ /
Important numbers		/ /	/ /	/ /	/ /
Isotopes	12	/ /	/ /	/ /	/ /
(d) Bonding, structure & properties					
Bonding		/ /	/ /	/ /	/ /
Structure - discrete molecules	13	/ /	/ /	/ /	/ /
Structure - covalent network lattices	14	/ /	/ /	/ /	/ /
Structure - ionic lattices		/ /	/ /	/ /	/ /
Structure - metallic lattices		/ /	/ /	/ /	/ /
Properties	15	/ /	/ /	/ /	/ /
Conductivity		/ /	/ /	/ /	/ /
Melting points and boiling points		/ /	/ /	/ /	/ /
Solubility		/ /	/ /	/ /	/ /
Electrolysis	16	/ /	/ /	/ /	/ /
(e) Chemical symbolism					
Formulae: prefixes, using the data booklet,		/ /	/ /	/ /	/ /
group ions, Roman numerals and brackets		/ /	/ /	/ /	/ /
(f) The mole	17				
Number of moles		/ /	/ /	/ /	/ /
Masses to moles and moles to masses		/ /	/ /	/ /	/ /
Using balanced equations		/ /	/ /	/ /	/ /

Name:

Unit 1 (Int 2) Study/Check sheet

Unit 2   Carbon Compounds   Intermediate 2

Contents	Page	Commenced	Completed	Revision 1	Revision 2
(a) Fuels	18				
Combustion		/ /	/ /	/ /	/ /
Fossil fuels		/ /	/ /	/ /	/ /
Some burning issues		/ /	/ /	/ /	/ /
Fractional distillation	19	/ /	/ /	/ /	/ /
(b) Nomenclature and structural formulae	20				
Hydrocarbons		/ /	/ /	/ /	/ /
Alkanes		/ /	/ /	/ /	/ /
Branched-chain alkanes		/ /	/ /	/ /	/ /
Alkenes		/ /	/ /	/ /	/ /
Cycloalkanes	21	/ /	/ /	/ /	/ /
Isomers		/ /	/ /	/ /	/ /
Alkanols		/ /	/ /	/ /	/ /
Alkanoic acids	22	/ /	/ /	/ /	/ /
Esters		/ /	/ /	/ /	/ /
Test yourself!		/ /	/ /	/ /	/ /
(c) Reactions of carbon compounds	23				
Addition reactions		/ /	/ /	/ /	/ /
Cracking		/ /	/ /	/ /	/ /
Ethanol - in alcoholic beverages		/ /	/ /	/ /	/ /
Ethanol - a chemical in great demand	24	/ /	/ /	/ /	/ /
Making and breaking esters		/ /	/ /	/ /	/ /
(d) Plastics and synthetic fibres	25				
Uses		/ /	/ /	/ /	/ /
Addition polymerisation	26	/ /	/ /	/ /	/ /
Condensation polymerisation		/ /	/ /	/ /	/ /
(e) Natural products	27				
Carbohydrates		/ /	/ /	/ /	/ /
Reactions of carbohydrates	28	/ /	/ /	/ /	/ /
Proteins	29	/ /	/ /	/ /	/ /
Fats and oils	30	/ /	/ /	/ /	/ /

Unit 3   Acids, Bases and Metals   Intermediate 2

Contents	Page	Commenced	Completed	Revision 1	Revision 2
(a) Acids and Bases	31				
The pH scale		/ /	/ /	/ /	/ /
Sources of some acids and alkalis		/ /	/ /	/ /	/ /
Common acids and alkalis		/ /	/ /	/ /	/ /
Water, aqueous solutions, ions and pH	32	/ /	/ /	/ /	/ /
Chemical equilibrium		/ /	/ /	/ /	/ /
Concentration		/ /	/ /	/ /	/ /
Strong and weak acids	33	/ /	/ /	/ /	/ /
Strong and weak bases		/ /	/ /	/ /	/ /
(b) Salt preparation					
Reactions of acids (neutralisation)		/ /	/ /	/ /	/ /
Neutralisation at work!		/ /	/ /	/ /	/ /
Salts and hydrogen from acids	34	/ /	/ /	/ /	/ /
Acid rain		/ /	/ /	/ /	/ /
Volumetric titrations		/ /	/ /	/ /	/ /
Naming salts	35	/ /	/ /	/ /	/ /
Precipitation	36	/ /	/ /	/ /	/ /
Ionic equations and spectator ions		/ /	/ /	/ /	/ /
(c) Metals					
Electricity from chemicals		/ /	/ /	/ /	/ /
An Electrochemical Series	37	/ /	/ /	/ /	/ /
Displacement reactions and redox		/ /	/ /	/ /	/ /
Hydrogen in the electrochemical series	38	/ /	/ /	/ /	/ /
Metal/metal ion cells		/ /	/ /	/ /	/ /
Half-cells without metals		/ /	/ /	/ /	/ /
More balanced redox equations	39	/ /	/ /	/ /	/ /
Electrolysis cells		/ /	/ /	/ /	/ /
Reactions of metals	40	/ /	/ /	/ /	/ /
Metals and oxygen		/ /	/ /	/ /	/ /
Metals and water		/ /	/ /	/ /	/ /
Metals and acid		/ /	/ /	/ /	/ /
A reactivity series	41	/ /	/ /	/ /	/ /
Metal ores		/ /	/ /	/ /	/ /
Corrosion	42	/ /	/ /	/ /	/ /
The chemistry of rusting		/ /	/ /	/ /	/ /
Preventing corrosion	43	/ /	/ /	/ /	/ /
Protective metal layers		/ /	/ /	/ /	/ /
Anti-corrosion methods in action		/ /	/ /	/ /	/ /
Sacrificial protection		/ /	/ /	/ /	/ /
Cathodic protection		/ /	/ /	/ /	/ /

Name:

Unit 3 (Int 2) Study/Check sheet

Course Assessment   Chemistry (Intermediate 2)

Internal Assessment

"Well, now that I've done all that chemistry and passed all the performance criteria for the three outcomes in each of these three Units, have I done enough to pass my Intermediate 2 Chemistry course?"

Outcome 1: demonstrate knowledge and understanding of course content from a closed book test

Outcome 2: solve problems related to course content

Outcome 3: collect and analyse information obtained by experiment and present a report

External Assessment

"I'm afraid not! There is still a two-hour external examination paper which will have knowledge and understanding and problem solving questions from each Unit and even some on the prescribed practical experiments!"

One written examination paper (2 hour)

Section 1 (30 marks)   Multiple Choice questions (25)
Grid questions (5)

Section 2 (50 marks*)   Question and answer booklet (no choice of questions)

* Approximately 10% of the marks will relate to the prescribed practical work

* The remainder of the marks will relate to knowledge and understanding and problem solving in the approximate ratio of 3 : 2

It is very important that you have a sound knowledge of these experiments.

Experimental details, e.g individual chemicals and types of apparatus used, will vary within schools and colleges for a few of these practical exercises but this display should remind you of the chemistry involved.

Effect of concentration on reaction rate

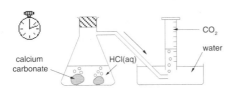

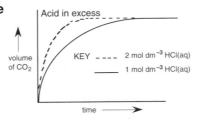

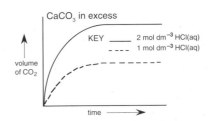

Effect of temperature on reaction rate

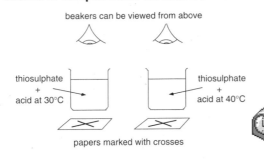

Testing for unsaturation

The presence of C=C bonds in a molecule are identified by the very fast loss in colour of the pale brown bromine solution.

An addition reaction has taken place.

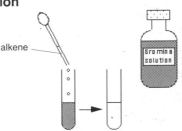

Hydrolysis of starch

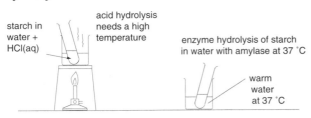

Cracking

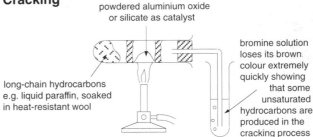

powdered aluminium oxide or silicate as catalyst

long-chain hydrocarbons e.g. liquid paraffin, soaked in heat-resistant wool

bromine solution loses its brown colour extremely quickly showing that some unsaturated hydrocarbons are produced in the cracking process

Factors affecting cell voltage

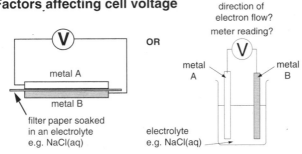

Electrolysis

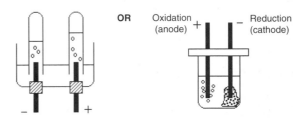

Positive ions are discharged at the negative electrode (cathode) and negative ions are discharged at the positive electrode (anode).

Preparation of a salt

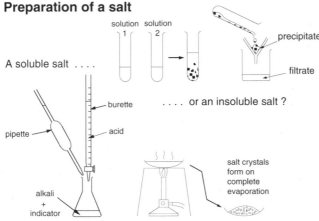

Reactions of metals with oxygen

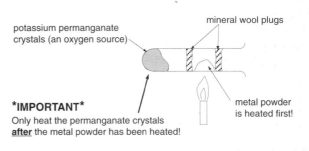

IMPORTANT
Only heat the permanganate crystals **after** the metal powder has been heated!

An order of reactivity for metals may be established according to the energy released during the reaction with oxygen.